A WHITE MAN'S JOURNEY TO A NORTHEASTERN AMERICAN INDIAN FAITH
and Its Relevance Today

Replicated Northeastern American Indian Village, Early White-Contact
(at the Institute for American Indian Studies)

Dedication

To the Creator, for allowing me the vision to see this heaven on Earth and to serve my fellow human beings and all Creation in whatever special way I can.

To my dear friends, all the wild creatures of this Earth—You are always with me, and I will never feel alone.

To Father Sun and Mother Earth, who greet me at the dawn of each precious day.

To all the "human angels" in my life—May you all be blessed, as you have blessed me.

To my dear family—You have brought such joy into my life. I love you all.

To my five book angles: my wife Debbie; and my editors: Chez Liley, Beth Walker, Jane Lahr, and Jane Bernstein—Without your understanding and warm support, this book would never have become a reality.

To all Native American elder-teachers, who, over hundreds and thousands of years, have kept alive the oral traditions of your Nations.

To the reader—Bless you for joining my earthly family. May the Creator make your stay on Mother Earth be the heaven that is mine.

In Grateful and Loving Memory

To my two very special elder-teachers:

Adelphena Logan of the Onondaga Nation of the Iroquois Confederacy, our family's beloved "grandmother,"

and Keewaydinoquay of the Ojibway Nation of the Anishinaabeg Confederacy, my inspiration in so many activities of life.

My faith is the faith you taught me. You continue to guide, support, and encourage me as I follow my life-path of service to the Creator, Mother Earth, and my fellow human beings.

Contents

List of Illustrations

Foreword

My husband Dave Richmond and I have known Ned Swigart for nearly thirty years, and it has been a wonderful journey. We met in the late 1970s, when the first phase of Ned's dream—his vision—had just been completed: The Institute for America Indian Studies* was open. At the time, I was co-founder of a new Native agency, American Indians for Development; and the Indian Institute director, Richard Davis, invited me to be one of the consultants advising the board of directors in the development of programs and tours for the public and school groups visiting this beautiful facility nestled in the hills of northwestern Connecticut.

On the occasion of one of our visits to the Institute, Ned greeted us, beaming as he guided us through the building. It is not often that one's vision or dream becomes a reality. This man's vision gave birth to a museum that provides a presence and a voice for the indigenous people of the area. It is more than a research and education center. Ned's vision brought together Algonquian Native people from throughout southern New England—Schaghticoke, Golden Hill Paugussett, Pequot, Narragansett, Wampanoag—and the Iroquois from throughout upper New York State, especially Onondaga, Seneca, and Akwesasne Mohawk.

The Indian Institute is more than just a building to house the hundreds of artifacts excavated by archaeologists. It incorporates the values, beliefs, and worldview of Native peoples throughout the Northeast. It reflects the lessons that Ned's elder-teachers taught him so well, especially Adelphena Logan and Keewaydinoquay. Del, a member of the Onondaga Tribe-Nation, helped to raise the funds to build the Institute. She was there for the groundbreaking ceremonies in 1974 when she assisted in removing the first symbolic shovelful of

---

* The Institute for American Indian Studies was originally called the American Indian Archaeological Institute.

earth and was present again when the building officially opened on July 1, 1975. Her contributions and dedication did not stop there. Del directed the building of an authentic longhouse in the Institute's primary classroom. In addition, she both donated as well as made many of the furnishings that are still there today. My husband and I have very fond memories of spending time in that beautiful and all-inspiring lodge. It was and continues to be a wonderful and valuable teaching tool. Keewaydinoquay was another beloved elder-teacher whose beliefs and values Ned respected so much. A traditional elder of the Anishinaabeg [Ojibway] people of the Great Lakes area, she was medicine woman, a teacher, an ethnobotanist, and an author. One of the most important lessons she shared with Ned was that medicines were more than something put in a bottle. They represented an attitude, a belief that plants and animals are the brothers and sisters, the relatives to humankind.

Taking the lead from these two wonderful Native elders, Ned has adopted a philosophy shared by all his Native teachers: What good is knowledge if it is not shared? This is the foundation on which the Institute for American Indian Studies was built.

Trudie Lamb Richmond, Schaghticoke
David Richmond, Akwesasne Mohawk
Ledyard, Connecticut
2008

Introduction

In late July of 1984, a wise Aztec elder-teacher called the Maestro gazed at me in his extremely perceptive way. Through an interpreter, he said to me, "Your heart has been given to cure people. You are destined for a great mission to help all people. You are a guide. You are a communicator between the world of spirits and the world of humans."

Twenty-five years later, the Maestro's prediction has come to fruition for me with this sharing of the northeastern American Indian faith. This story is not written in conventional book form. Instead, it is offered to you in the "Old Way" of the oral tradition used by Native Americans to pass on their heritage. This is the way I learned Indian faith and culture from my northeastern American Indian elder-teachers, and it is the way I, as an elder now, wish to pass it on to all of our brothers and sisters who may profit from its wisdom. As you read, I ask you to imagine that we are walking through the Institute for American Indian Studies and talking together.

"What we do not share, we lose," Native-American elder-teacher Black Hawk once said. Because I believe that the traditional northeastern American Indian culture and religious beliefs offer so much of value for future generations of human beings everywhere, and because I believe that the potential loss of these would be catastrophic, I invite you to come walk with me. In the Old Way of the oral tradition (with the help of some "new way" tools), I will share my personal life-journey to the Ojibway-Onondaga and northeastern American Indian faith, and I will show how this faith has brought me—a white man—inner serenity, contentment, and strength in my later years. These qualities allow me to experience a positive life-view and life-path despite the social, religious, and ecological crises the world faces today. This faith has meant so much to me. I believe I am alive today by the Creator's Will to offer to you the story that follows, and I serve the Creator as I am bidden.

Therefore, come walk with me as I share a life-path that has given me the ultimate blessings of this faith: a vision that led to the creation of the Institute for American Indian Studies, and the opportunity to relate this story. Come walk with me as I tell of the almost unbelievable series of miracles and human angels that the Creator provided—and still provides—to assist, sustain, and encourage me and others who believe in this vision of cultural sharing and understanding.

In telling this story, I do not seek to prove Indian lineage. I claim only a long and close association with Indian people of many nations. Nor will I ask you, the reader, to become an Indian. Moreover, I do not portray my faith as that of a specific northeastern American Indian nation, although most of my core beliefs have come from my Ojibway (Algonquin) and, to a lesser degree, my Onondaga (Iroquois) elder-teachers. Others, far more knowledgeable than I, share the precious information of their unique tribal heritage as they are so moved. Instead, I offer my beliefs from a deeply personal perspective, which is, in fact, a basic tenet of the northeastern Native American path to faith.

I make no excuses, for I have learned over my long lifetime—I am seventy-eight years old—that you are what you believe, and I believe with my whole heart in the traditional northeastern American Indian Old Way. After all, one does not have to be Chinese to practice Buddhism, Jewish to observe Judaism, European or North American to embrace Christianity, or of Arab descent to follow Islamic beliefs.

I invite you to walk with me as I share the "good news" of the northeastern Native American path, even as I ask myself "Why me?"

Northeastern Native Americans and others have supported me in this venture, and two elders—the Maestro and an Onondaga woman—have both prophesized my sharing, in a written form, the information I have been taught with the people of the world.

I pray that by reading this book, you too may come to realize new meaning and direction in your own life and faith. I pray that you may become aware of the Creator's gifts of miracles and human angels to help you realize your unique purpose, and to help you create a better world for yourself, for all humankind, and for our planet Earth. If this book should also help any northeastern Native Americans to renew or maintain their faith and sustain them in following their own life-paths, then I will be doubly blessed.

Crazy Horse, Chief of the Minneconjou Band of the Oglala Sioux Nation, once said, "A very great vision is needed, and the one who has it must follow it as the eagle seeks the deepest blue of the sky." Indeed, very great visions *are* needed if we are to discover and act on what is meaningful and important, not just to human beings, but also to this planet on which we live. I am honored to share my vision with you.

Chapter 1
The Oral Tradition and a Vision

It is a beautiful fall day in the New England hills, and you drive your car into the parking lot at the Institute for American Indian Studies in Washington, Connecticut. I walk from the main building to greet you. You have heard of our museum and its message, and perhaps you have come here because you are interested in the American Indian way of life, or perhaps for no better reason than to find something to do—a family outing—on a weekend afternoon. As you all climb out of your car, I welcome you. I will be your guide today. I will share my message with you in the Old Way: the oral tradition by which untold generations of Native American people have passed on their faith and their culture. This is how my Native American elder-teachers passed this message to me.

First, by way of introduction, let me tell you briefly about myself. I was born in March of 1931 in Milwaukee, Wisconsin. My earliest memories are of summers with my family in the northeastern part of the state. We lived in a primitive cabin with no electricity, running water, heat, or indoor plumbing, near the Potawatomi-Ojibway Indian settlement that was later to become the Partridge Lake Indian Reservation. During the 1930s and until the end of World War II, this part of Wisconsin was a largely unsettled "wilderness" with relatively few white people residing there. Some Native Americans, like those at Partridge Lake, still lived in wigwams in the traditional way during the summers but had switched to log cabins near white settlements in the winters. My father and grandfather were good friends of the local Indian people, particularly the family of Chief John Escanaba, who lived on Partridge Lake with his relatives and others who had chosen to follow him as their chief. It was the Escanaba family who introduced me, a shy young boy from the farm country twenty miles north of Milwaukee, to their oneness with nature. As an only child with a

1

mother suffering from serious health issues and a father who worked long hours in the city, I spent most of my time roaming the out-of-doors with the plants and animals as my companions. Therefore, this example of the Indian way—their traditions and faith, their close connection with Mother Earth and all living things—was much like my own experience and, over time, formed the philosophy by which I now choose to live.

Anna Escanaba, Ojibway,
Northeastern Wisconsin (1911)

After the death of my father in 1945 and my mother's subsequent marriage to a childhood sweetheart, I moved east to Connecticut in 1947. Here, becoming part of my step-father's world, with all the distractions of the suburban/urban Fairfield-Southport-New York area, and attending the Hotchkiss School in Lakeville, Connecticut, I was temporarily submerged in a new social and predominantly Christian lifestyle. Nonetheless, I always found opportunities to escape, and spent as much time as I could in the summertime fishing, canoeing, hiking, and camping in the wilderness areas of northern Maine. I met Native American people in the East, but most were living in cities. These city dwellers were not like the Wisconsin Indians I had known, who were still largely able to follow their ancestors' Ojibway and Potawatomi traditions. Instead they were largely a mixture of many Native American nations and often, at that time, largely immersed in the mainstream American cultural lifestyle. However, I was also fortunate to meet people, mostly Schaghticoke, who were still members of a tribal entity and lived on reservations in Connecticut in their endeavor to continue living in the Old Way. This was difficult for them, however, surrounded as they were by a white man's world with its rewards, temptations, cultural differences, and racial discrimination.

During my later college and graduate years, I pursued my interest in and association with the out-of-doors by getting a masters degree in Conservation at Yale University and a doctorate in Conservation and Education at Columbia Pacific University. I brought my lifetime passion for nature and my knowledge to my teaching at the Gunnery School in Washington, Connecticut, as well as to my work for the Massachusetts and National Audubon Societies and the Housatonic Valley (Watershed) Association. I also lectured, consulted on, and wrote about environmental concerns.

From time to time during these years I tried unsuccessfully to trace what I believed was my Indian ancestry. Finally, in my thirties, I came to realize this wasn't necessary, for my apparent life-path followed the northeastern American Indian way, regardless of whether I had Indian blood. This was a major turning point in my life.

Thus it was that when I reached the age of thirty-nine, I was prepared to experience an extraordinary event: a vision, in the northeastern American Indian manner, during daylight hours and without prior warning or provocation of any kind. The experience changed my life forever.

Let us remain here by your car for a few minutes more while I share this vision with you.

On a hot summer morning in early July of 1970, I was kneeling in our vegetable garden in Washington, Connecticut, weeding the carrot patch. Suddenly, as I looked up, my wife Debbie, our three children, and I had become American Indians and our house a wigwam. Then the Creator's words flooded me. I must give up my present, comfortable, secure life, and create a northeastern regional Indian museum. Its purpose would be to rescue, preserve, and share over 10,000 years of the largely unknown history of a Native American people who lived in this part of the world with a philosophy of caring for Mother Earth rather than pillaging her, as we currently seemed to be doing. After a moment, the vision ended.

As I thought about this experience and tried to articulate it to family and close friends, I became increasingly overcome by its ramifications: The museum was to be dedicated to the sharing of a northeastern American Indian culture that could offer a much-needed, viable alternative to the social, political, religious, and ecological crises affecting the modern world! The project also had to be undertaken immediately; otherwise, rapidly increasing development would forever eliminate the opportunity to rescue and share the culture. Almost everywhere that white colonists chose as the very best places to settle, pre-white Indians had preceded them for the same reasons. Many, if not most, of the Indians' major cities lay under our cities and their towns under our towns. Those potentially revealing large Indian settlement sites had already been destroyed long ago. Time was running out for rescuing what we could from the mainly rural sites that remained. They would be inadequate for exploring the complexity of life in the great Native cities but were still meaningful examples of what Indian culture was like.

In my vision the Creator had assured me that everything would be "all right" for my wife and me, and we interpreted this as applying to the continued personal and financial wellbeing of our family. To most of the people I knew, this life-change filled with so many potential problems seemed absurd—even crazy—to consider, and almost every non-Indian person told me so in no uncertain terms. However, I knew in my heart that I had no choice but to pursue my vision, for it had to be the Creator's Will; but these negative comments did reinforce my lingering misgivings about the effect this change of lifestyle might have on the other members of my immediate family. After long and soul-searching discussions with my wife, we agreed that I must indeed begin to give up the long-term financial and psychological security of my professions as a teacher, consultant, lecturer, and writer. I must instead move into unfamiliar territory, following new career paths in which I had little or no experience. These were fundraising, museum management, and administration.

I shared this vision shortly thereafter with a good friend, Sidney A. Hessel, who was retired and also lived in the town of Washington. He was a scholar with encyclopedic knowledge of many subjects including the natural world, archaeology, and what was known about the history of Indian people at the time. Sid accepted the idea of this regional Indian center unreservedly but with an innate caution that was his strength. He joined me as a co-founder of the facility; and during the remainder of his short time left with us on this Earth, he would become the one person who could slow me down when he felt I was progressing too fast and encourage me when I got discouraged.

When we finally decided to make public the idea of the creation of a museum in 1971, nearly all of the non-profit professionals with whom we spoke were forthright in their opinions. They advised us that:

"This could not be done."

"The time was wrong."

"The money was not available because the museum was in a rural area an hour from the nearest cities and half an hour from the nearest towns."

We heard every possible argument about why we should not proceed with the project and could not succeed if we did. Even my faithful wife, outwardly totally supportive, later admitted succinctly that she believed: "You were out of your mind." None of this deterred Sid and me from moving forward with the project, however, for we were both fully committed to it at this point.

Ned Swigart and Sidney Hessel,
Co-founders of the Institute for American Indian Studies

As the fundraiser-organizer designate, I began to try to raise money and put together, with Sid's help and advice, a board of directors. The rest is history. The dreamer (me) in Washington, Connecticut (the town that was too small and in the middle of nowhere), raised almost $500,000 in one year and, in five years, close to $2,000,000 (an amount that could not be raised) from people who cared (but weren't supposed to), first locally, then from all over the United States, and eventually from five foreign countries!

As an exclamation point to my vision, this "impossible dream," an additional dramatic, corroborative event occurred a year later. When Debbie and I plowed our vegetable garden the next spring, I discovered artifacts and debitage (waste debris from artifact construction) from a 4,000-year-old campsite that was exposed for the first time right under the very spot where I had been kneeling when I had had this vision the year before!

With the necessary funds raised in less than three years, in 1974 we began to build the Institute for American Indian Studies that you will visit today. The original facility consisted of a 3,000-square-foot, circular, state-of-the-art museum and research building with temperature and humidity controls and the best current alarm technology. The siding was constructed of board-and-batten (wood) and split-faced (ridged) cinder block. Inside, the space was open to the ceiling and fall-leaf colors highlighted a largely natural wood finish. The Institute and its beautiful and unusual design were an immediate success.

In only four years the board of directors had met our ten- and twenty-year goals: We had thirty full- and part-time staff; we had essentially doubled our collection size and were running out of space; we had added two wings, one as big as the original building. During the late 1990s, as the demand on our programs and facilities continued to escalate, we added a separate building twice the size of the original one. The lower floor was underground with the most modern facilities for our collections, and the upper floor consisted of research and education libraries, offices, and a large meeting room.

As for me personally, my complete career change and the potential financial challenges of educating and caring for our growing family went surprisingly well. When needed, scholarship money was available for our children and our guardian and foster children, and everything was truly "all right," as the Creator had promised. Thirty-four years later, the Indian Institute is still flourishing, still growing in size, and still offering vital education, research, and curatorial services for which we have been recognized both nationally and internationally over the years.

Chapter 2

Welcome to the Institute:
Meet Our Elders

Come walk with me. Let us move into a different world, that of the northeastern American Indian.

Notice, as we walk, that you are surrounded by nature, which the northeastern American Indians recognized themselves as an integral part of. Every plant and every animal that you see and hear has its special place in the natural world and its own significance in the grand scheme of Indian life. For example, the willows by the edge of the parking lot are quick to grow on disturbed, moist, sunlit land; and their roots hold the soil to prevent erosion. Their bark, when boiled, was a source of aspirin to Native peoples before the era of modern drugs, and their flowers—"pussy willows," we call them—are an early sign of spring. Ahead of us on the left, we see red clusters of the berries of the sumac. Sumac grows best in sunlit but dry land around forest edges and in swales in open fields. The fruit can be picked and preserved by hanging in a dry place. From sumac fruit, generations of Native peoples made a tasty lemonade-like beverage that was a much-needed source of vitamin C, especially in winter when fresh fruit was not available.

As we approach the walkway leading to the museum, you will see on either side two of the three trees which are the most important to the Ojibway for religious, medicinal, and technological uses. On the left is the white cedar, the Ojibway "Grandmother Tree," and on the right is the white birch, their "Grandfather Tree." The white cedar is a favorite winter food for deer and has a multitude of human uses, the most special involving the cedar oil produced by steaming new buds and leaves, where the oil is most concentrated. Cedar oil is used as a gift from the Creator to anoint a child as it enters this world and to anoint a person who is departing this world. The white birch in the driveway circle is important to many northeastern nations. It is a tree of numerous miraculous uses. When all is cold and wet around you and you desperately need a fire to warm you, the birch bark—sodden as it may be—will burst into flame when a spark touches it. If you are hungry, this same bark can be folded into the shape of a bowl and suspended over your fire; without catching fire, the birch bark bowl will allow you to warm your food.

Institute for American Indian Studies, Education and Exhibit Building

As we continue toward the building, let us stop and attempt to feel the special Aura surrounding this place. The Aura, a gift from and part of the Creator, surrounds you and becomes part of you here. This is because the land upon which the museum rests has been blessed with prayers and offerings of tobacco by many of the Indian elders of different nations when they have visited us. People of all persuasions who are sensitive to this Aura comment about it. Awareness of the spiritual quality of the Indian Institute as a whole has now spread to a point where Native Americans are visiting our center in growing numbers as part of their own Creator-inspired life-quest or death-quest. And we rejoice in this.

Notice the building as we begin to move up the front walk. It was constructed using a traditional Indian design: the shape of a wigwam-teepee. This configuration honors the circle, in which all things Indian take place. The circle is the bedrock of Indian philosophy and culture. Notice, also, the earth tones of the building and the way it blends in with, rather than overwhelms, the natural world all around it. We had originally planned to put it underground so as not to disturb the profound serenity of this site. However, in digging the foundation we immediately ran into ledge and so had to build aboveground. We are now glad that that part of our dream was not to be. (Notice, the Creator can say no as well as yes to some parts of any life-plan.) We are overjoyed with our aboveground design because, even as we move up this front walk, the visual lessons in the building's shape, its colors, and its composition of simple, practical, local material are already making an impression upon us.

As we approach the large, glass entryway, I must ask a favor of you. From this moment on, try to imagine that you have been born into the Wolf Clan of a traditional northeastern American Indian nation. I am bringing you to this special place to learn more about the faith and culture of your Indian brothers and sisters. There are two things you must appreciate right away from an Indian perspective, and we give thanks to the Creator for them both: The first is that life is a gift. The second is that from the day you are born until the day you pass over, you are privileged to serve the Creator as a steward of all Creation. The Judeo-Christian religion has a similar tradition of stewardship, but this primary duty of these faiths has been largely lost. My hope is that humankind will regain this all-important sense of stewardship of all Creation, so important, still, in the core-faith of traditional Native American people.

Let us now pass through these entryway doors into the world of the traditional northeastern American Indian.

Notice, straight ahead of us is a stone object carved in the shape of a bird. This artifact was sculpted approximately 3,000 years ago out of banded slate, probably from the state of Michigan. The birdstone is the logo of our Indian Institute.

I have seen many extraordinary examples of this type of superb craftsmanship, so modern and sleek in its appearance. One thing always strikes me as I look at this style of carving: It represents what the carver sees in nature. Our birdstone clearly resembles a loon. Across the northern United States the loon is a messenger from the Creator and is

Birdstone

a clan symbol of political and cultural importance, but the use of the birdstone is still a mystery. We chose it as our logo because it reminds us of the long and continuing presence of Native American people in the Northeast and is a visible symbol of how much we have yet to learn about the intricacies of their past great cultures.

Let us now leave the foyer and move into the entry hall leading to our main exhibit room. Here, we are greeted by portraits of our honored Indian elder-teachers. These elders are the guardian spirits of our museum and the keepers of the knowledge that I am sharing with you. Let me introduce a few of them, these Native American elders, many of whom have now passed over to another level of existence but who have meant so much to their people, to the Indian Institute, and to me in my own personal growth toward a life of faith.

Notice the beautiful portrait on your left. This is the lasting image of our beloved friend and grandmother-figure to our children, Adelphena "Del" Logan, an Iroquois lady of the Onondaga Nation, teacher of the Old Way, and the Institute's first spiritual leader. She

Native American Elder-Teachers' Portraits in the Hall of Honor

passed over in 1978. Her portrait and all the others you see hanging on this wall were painted by David Wagner, a talented artist of Indian people and Indian life.

I am introducing Del to you first, not only because she had great knowledge and was a born teacher, but also because of a powerful truth she taught me long ago: that after one passes over to the spirit world, the Creator allows their spirit to return to Earth when needed. Del also assured me personally that the Creator would permit her always to "be there" for my family and for all of us at Institute. A year after Del passed over, Ella Thomas Sekatau (Narragansett), a former member of our Native American advisory board, elder-teacher, and friend, verified this as a belief she also shared; many elders of other Algonquin and Iroquois Nations in subsequent years have expressed the same belief to me.

On the right is Ken Mynter of the Mohican Nation, a historian of his people and a very special individual. When Del passed over before completing a new set of buckskins for me, it was Ken who recognized my own need to have the precious reminder of my Wisconsin days, and, without a word, he took on this task as a gift from Del's spirit. Ken, who has since passed over, was a loyal member of our Native American advisory committee and did everything he could to share a culture and faith of great worth and promise.

Looking to the left again, the next person I wish to introduce is Keewaydinoquay of the Ojibway Algonquin Nation, whose teachings have had the greatest impact on me. She corroborated the experiences I had with the Escanaba family as a child, and taught me the basic tenants of her faith and the profound knowledge of her culture that I find so inspirational. Kee passed over in 1999.

Trudie Lamb Richmond of the Schaghticoke Nation is next. She is still an active teacher of her faith. With the passing over of Del, Trudie slipped into the key roles Del had so ably assumed. With quiet dignity, she became the spiritual leader that the Indian Institute needed to continue to move forward in our quest to share our message of understanding and faith during and after her distinguished tenure here.

Gladys Tantaquidgeon of the Mohegan Nation, whose portrait also hangs on your left-hand side, recently passed over. She was a medicine woman for her people, small in stature but a giant in terms of her dedication and ability to communicate the ways of her Mohegan heritage. Her important role serving the Creator and her people touched an amazing three centuries—she passed over in the fall of 2005 at the age of 106.

Gladys Tantaquidgeon, Mohegan, Elder-Teacher Portrait in the Hall of Honor (Painting by David Wagner)

There are so many others whom we honor on this wall with thanksgiving to the Creator for all they have done and are doing as guardians of our Indian Institute and as the original elder-teachers for all who come to learn in this place. The spirit of these people and their teachings while they were here with me on Mother Earth echo in my mind, and it is their knowledge and their stories that I will share with you today.

Notice the serenity and strength of these elders, and the way they talk to us with their expressive eyes; it is a trademark of the power of their faith. These elders have passed on to us the history of their people, largely by word of mouth, carrying on this legacy from as far back as it can be remembered. The oral tradition is still practiced, and together you and I are keeping it alive today. Fortunately, the northeastern American Indian history, culture, and faith are now also being recorded more and more in written form, as well. This written record is offered, not only for the sake of Indian people who are maintaining or returning to their traditional life-ways, but also for non-Indians who wish to learn the vital message of this cultural alternative to Western thinking.

Trudie Lamb Richmond has spoken and written so eloquently on the subject of the oral tradition. As we move slowly and reverently between the rows of our elder-teachers, let me quote Trudie:

> When we were young it was our Grandmother who gathered us around to tell us of many things: of how the world began; of where we came from; of why we must respect all living things; of the wonders of the universe. She always told us of the old ways. And when we were told these things, these truths, we searched her face of many wrinkles and believed she must have been there, way back then, in the beginning—so vivid were her words and the pictures she created in our mind's eye. It was only when we were much older that we realized that this was the way of the elders. The words were the traditions being passed down from the grandmothers and grandfathers.
>
> What is remembered is the influence of Grandmother's words and the way these words guided our lives. We didn't know then what we have come to know now: that in the beginning there was nothing but the Word, and it was all-powerful. It is life itself. And the Word breathed life into Man. To the native peoples of North America the Thought and the Word were sacred and all-powerful, and from the Word there developed the oral tradition to carry forth and sustain life. It began the cycle of life and from this evolved our ceremonies to sustain our close relationship with the environment and to maintain the balance and the harmony with the universe. The hypnotic quality of Grandmother's carefully selected words healed us, cured us, strengthened and enriched our lives—which we were committed to pass on [sic.][1]

The Algonquin and Iroquoian teachers in the Hall of Elders instruct us that a supreme strength of the oral tradition is that it is passed soul-spirit to soul-spirit, not face-to-face, where what you mean can literally be hidden by your expression (a mask, as we call it in psychological terms). Nor does the oral tradition involve e-mail, written letters, fax, or telephone. The oral tradition is a soul-spirit to soul-spirit communication, so one must always speak the truth to an Indian; otherwise the words will be recognized as false since the soul-spirit cannot be hidden by the mask we Westerners can wear. As a result, the cultural traditions of their nations are passed on by elder-teachers with remarkable accuracy.

That said, I and many of my Indian teachers may very well see this faith from slightly different perspectives than other teachers even in the same village, as my Ojibway teacher Keewaydinoquay often reminded me. I am sure this is right, for while the basic tenets of traditional Indian philosophy have remained largely unchanged, slight shifts of focus and detail may have occurred over time and may still be occurring because of each elder-teacher's unique life-path. Kee often told me she believed that, as essential as the integrity of the oral tradition was in passing on her heritage, she experienced a unique life-journey and each person in her village and nation did the same. Thus, she believed her personal perspective and those of her people could not help but influence the way she and they shared their heritage with others. For instance, Kee told me that she was taught, and had even put into print, that the journey on the Path of Souls to the Land of Souls (known as "Heaven" in the Judeo-Christian tradition) took three days and three nights, whereas another Ojibway elder-teacher whom we both respected greatly had stated in print that it took four days and four nights to reach this same Land of Souls.

Del Logan also acknowledged that the long association of a number of Iroquois people with early Christian missionaries, and the outward similarities that she and others saw over the years between Christianity and her own faith, may have subtly left its mark on her people's collective thinking and thus on their oral tradition. As she said to us on several occasions, her Indian faith and the Christian faith she was taught were different—but not *that* different. She personally could accept the Christian faith and still maintain her "Indian-ness." Both cultures worshiped a single God—the Creator. Both believed in prophets, Jesus to Christians and Deganwidah to the Iroquois. Both believed that God was present in all human beings—the Christian concept of the Holy Spirit (which is present in all Creation, in the Iroquois faith). Both believed in the duty of stewardship of our world and in a concept of Heaven. And, of great importance, both believed that ordinary objects, like Indian tobacco and Christian bread and grape juice or wine, could be ritually transformed to become sacred Indian tobacco and the body and blood of Christ during a Christian communion service. Del suggested this is how the oral tradition could be affected by outside influences.

Elder-teachers practicing the oral tradition not only had to have excellent memories for historical facts and a charismatic way of delivering information, but also, like Del, they may have had to learn a number of different languages to communicate with others. Del, like all members of the Iroquois Confederacy, had to learn eight languages: English and seven languages within the confederacy—separate languages for each of the six nations (Mohawk, Oneida, Onondaga, Cayuga, Seneca, and Tuscarora), plus the Onondaga Court Language spoken by all participants at Councils and Grand Councils.

One interesting element about Del's own and other northeastern Indian languages is that they too can become teaching tools for a true teacher. For instance, when an occasion prompted me to use what I thought was an appropriate word, Del was quick to remind me, "Ned, we have no swear words in our traditional Iroquoian languages. They are a waste of time." And when one of our children became exasperated with another and shouted "shut up," Dell would admonish them, saying, "We Iroquois have no traditional word for 'shut up.' We are taught from a very early age that it is rude to interrupt and that we must listen carefully to what another person is saying until they are finished before we reply."

Now, come walk with me—and the elder-teachers who will be with us in spirit today—into our main exhibit hall where I will share what I have learned from them and other Native American mentors. Listen carefully, for what they have taught me, I believe, is true.

Chapter 3

The Creator of Us All

As we enter the main exhibit room, we begin this journey of faith with the Ojibway and Algonquin Creation myth. Keewaydinoquay, my Ojibway elder-teacher, has taught me about her people's story, which has a number of common elements with other northeastern and New England Algonquin Native American nations. The Great Spirit or Great Mystery of the Ojibway (God of other world religions) is the Creator of our universe, our planet, and all other things. According to the Ojibway, there was a great flood at the time of Creation. Turtle offered his dry back for the new earth, and Muskrat recovered a piece of the earth at the bottom of the water and placed it on Turtle's back. This became Mother Earth. Mother Earth was named Mother because underground rivers are her veins, the water on Earth is her blood, and from her come all living things. On her surface there are four sacred directions: east, south, north, and west. After Mother Earth was formed, the Gitche Manitou (Great Spirit) took four parts of her—earth, wind, fire, and water—and blew into them, using the Sacred Shell. Man was created in this way. Gitche Manitou then lowered man to Mother Earth to become part of Her, to live in brotherhood with all that surrounded him, and to become the Creator's steward in all things. On Earth he became Original (Native American) Man, and the Anishinaabeg, the original known name of the Ojibway, and all other Native American groups were descended from this being. As apocryphal as this (and other religions' Creation stories) may be, there is much in this narrative that forms the bedrock of Ojibway faith and culture.

Now let us share a very special Ojibway prayer that Keewaydinoquay's grandmother taught her long ago and that people such as myself say at appropriate times every day. This Prayer of the Seven Directions will ready us for the great adventure we will share today. It is a reminder to Ojibway people of their Creation story and thus is one of the most sacred of their prayers. In it, we acknowledge the four sacred directions and then we recognize three more all-important reminders, also integral to the Creation story: looking up toward the Creator, down to Mother Earth, and inward to the very center of our being. I do not give the exact method or the specific Indian words for this prayer, as they are a sacred and private part of Ojibway life. But this general message, shared by Ojibway elder-teachers with non-Indian people in English, is clear and powerful as it is.

Let us now offer this sacred prayer together.

First, we must approach the Creator with humility and gratitude. We gently rub our palms together until we feel an energy being generated between them, and we open our palms to the sky, releasing this energy upward to the Creator in thanksgiving.

Then with arms extended from our waist, we face the east, the "direction of whiteness," the source of light, of innocence and of new beginnings, and we share our prayers to the spirits of the east out loud so they may be heard.

We then turn and face the south with arms still extended. The south is the "direction of greenness," from which gentle, warm winds and soft rains make plants grow. This direction also gives us creativity, and we share our prayers to the spirits of the south out loud so they may be heard.

We then turn to face the west, arms extended. The west is the "direction of redness," the path our Grandfather Sun takes every day, the direction we begin to follow at birth, and the direction our ancestors take when passing over. The west is also the land where the spirits of our ancestors are, and we share our prayers to the spirits of the west out loud so they may be heard.

We then turn and face the north, arms extended. The north is the "direction of blackness," the "cold-blower" that gives strength, that is the Great Mystery of all Creation and the source of dreaming and becoming anew. We offer our prayers to the spirits of the north out loud so they may be heard.

We now cleanse our fingertips by rubbing them together, and then, arms extended at our waist, we slowly and with great reverence place our fingers and palms tenderly on Mother Earth, the provider of all we have. As we do this we share our prayers to the spirit of Mother Earth out loud so they may be heard.

We now reach upward once again, not in supplication but in thanksgiving, to offer our prayers out loud to the Great Mystery, the Creator above the sky and all around us, the Creator that created all things and is in all things, equally. As we do this, we share our prayers to the Great Mystery, the Creator, out loud so they may be heard.

Lastly we turn inward within ourselves, to where we are, filling a space in the universe that no one in the past, now, or in the future, will ever fill again, and we search for our "sun-trail" purpose and the ability to pursue it. We offer our prayers to the spirit within us out loud so they may be heard.

We finish this prayer of reminder and gratitude with the words "Balance is blessing, and blessing is balance. From all blessings comes balance."

As we now look about this beautiful room, please note that the exhibits here are presented by northeastern Native Americans the way *they* wish to share their faith and culture, by subjects of utmost importance to them over a long period of time, rather than by chronology, which is the approach used by almost all other museums. Notice the exhibits you see around the room, such as the one on our right: a Native American's attempt to describe the Creator-God and their existence of service to this Great Spirit here on Mother Earth. Other exhibits to our left include such concepts as Land, Exchange (the importance of trade as a social and uniting factor), Clay (an example of using Mother Earth), Living Space (and how it is tied to the Indian concept of land and its natural resources), Corn (representing plants), and Deer (representing animals).

Main Exhibit Room, Indian Culture from a Northeastern Indian Perspective

As we approach the exhibit which attempts to explain the Native American Creator-God, think on this a moment. How can we present the complicated and far reaching concept of the Great Spirit and the Great Spirit's involvement in every aspect of our lives in any exhibit, even here in this holy place? The subject is too important, vast, and complex for such a limited space; the artifacts available to help tell this story are too few and often not appropriate; and the artifact labels are brief, often not read, and therefore not very helpful. One way we attempt to explain this relationship of humans with the Creator is through the use of sacred masks and other materials that illustrate our relationship with the Creator. You will notice two recently carved Abnaki masks on display here. They are neither sacred nor replicas of those employed in the past, but examples of what might have been used. This is because some years ago Indian leaders requested that museums, including the Indian Institute, remove from exhibition the real masks and other objects most able to explain their faith and therefore considered sacred.

Del spoke eloquently about the use of sacred masks by Iroquoian people in her book *Memories of Sweet Grass:*

> Basically there are eight masks that have the greatest significance in our circle of life. These ceremonial masks are not used by everyone. Only those who have won the respect of the people participate in the services using the masks.
>
> Many non-Indians have regarded the masks with curiosity and misunderstanding. Non-Indians, particularly the settlers, have not recognized that the Indians have cultures. There are a few who befriended Indians on the basis of accepting their culture or wanting to truly understand. Gradually, non-Indians looked on Indians as curiosities: they wanted to bring cameras, to be amused—even in the area of religion. Our religion is sacred to us. Finally our Council had to decree that no non-Indian could view the religious ceremonies. Other religious groups do not like to be laughed at...Christians hold up a cross, they burn incense, and they use ashes. Why do people think the Indians are a funny, weird curiosity because they have masks and tobacco as symbols of life's lessons? Secret masked societies? Not secret to an Indian. Non-Indians have called the masks grotesque. They are magical to my people. The mask makes the person wearing it impersonal, so when we see the mask in the ceremony we think only of the lesson the mask represents.
>
> For an example, the most frequently seen mask in books and museums is the one the non-Indian calls "Crooked Face." To us this mask represents the greed and conceit, the selfishness and unreliability in man, and reminds us to discipline these qualities within ourselves.
>
> According to our lesson, the Creator came to earth to survey his Creation. As the Creator walked along, man came to his side and walked with him. The Creator asked man if there was anything that could be added for the comfort of man, or if there was anything more man needed. In his humble way the Creator

walked and talked with man. Man, however, did not recognize his companion and decided to show off his authority and power. Man refuted the Creator's words and told the Creator that he, man, had made all that there was. The more he talked, the more he boasted.

The Creator was disturbed by man's gloating, for this was not the way he intended man to be. The Creator decided to teach man a lesson, so he challenged man to move a mountain that was before them. They agreed that whoever could move the mountain the farthest would prove that that one was the Creator. Man agreed to the challenge, but wanted his challenger to go first.

The Creator knew that man could not be trusted, even though man had promised to turn his back and not look when his challenger took his turn at moving the mountain. When the Creator was moving the mountain, man did look to see how his opponent was doing it. As man turned to look, the mountain came rushing by, crushing man's face and distorting it.

In our services the wearer of this mask provides an impersonal reminder that we must be humble and honorable in our dealings with others and ourselves. The stories symbolized by our masks could be compared to the parables of the Christian Bible....

There are times masks are used for social occasions, too. The young boys make cloth masks with long noses, just like a clown, to cover their faces. This gives the youngsters a chance, especially the shy ones, to show how well they have learned the social dances. Because the masks make them "unknown" or "impersonal" to the viewers, the child is not self-conscious. He learns to participate equally, and that each mask-wearer has a contribution to make to the whole. This is a feature of the twenty-eight day mid-year ceremony.[2]

As to how these Iroquoian masks are created and become sacred, after a request has been made for a certain type to be carved, the highly skilled person who has been chosen to carve the mask offers the proper prayers and undergoes the necessary sweat-lodge purification ceremonies. The mask is then carved on a living basswood tree. This is to ensure that the Creator's Aura, in the tree, will empower the mask to make it sacred so it can serve its divine purpose. The mask, and a smaller replica of it, are then carefully separated from the tree, dried, and painted—red, if they are carved in the morning; black, if they are carved in the afternoon; even half red and half black, if the masks are carved over the noon period. If the tree subsequently dies, the large mask will lose its power and be discarded. If the tree lives, the large mask is blessed by the elders and hung in special lodges or other places, to be used in appropriate ceremonies. The smaller of the two masks, perhaps five inches tall, is then given away with deep affection by the carver to someone very special in their life.

Thus, as I hope you begin to understand now, in attempting to pass on the northeastern American Indian Old Way and share the belief in their Creator-God and their life of service, we must employ the Oral Tradition of Indian people as we are doing today instead of relying on insufficient and at times ineffective visual aids.

Who is this Creator, this Great Spirit that I have been taught to serve, love, and admire by my elder-teachers? There are different words used by northeastern American Indian people in their native languages for this Force. For instance, the word Mundu is used by the Mohegan people, and the Gitche Manitou by the Ojibway. Other northeastern nations may also use the word Manitou in some form. However, the most commonly used English translation for this concept is Great Spirit or Creator, and these are the words I will employ.

To northeastern Native Americans, this Great Spirit is not a figure in human form as other religions like Christianity and Judaism may suggest (for instance, Old Testament, Genesis, Chapter 1, verse 27: "So God created man in his own image"). The Great Spirit is, instead, an all encompassing Aura, or Invisible Cloud, that is present in all the inanimate and animate forms that make up our universe, including us. This means the Creator's Aura or Spirit is in the air, the sun, the rain, the rocks, the trees, and in all non-living and living things—equally!

Notice, if the Creator is in all these things equally, then we are obligated to treat Mother Earth and the entire natural world with the utmost respect as our family, for they are imbued, like us, with the Creator's Spirit. We humans on planet Earth are considered a very small part of this huge, intimately related universe we live in. We are, therefore, not the owners and rulers of the natural world, as we too often are led to believe by the Judeo-Christian tradition that most people in our country, and even some of our Native American population, follow now. We are born to serve our Creator as stewards, and we must remain, as the Great Spirit has created us—in harmony with Mother Earth and our universe—for our entire lives.

Consider some of the extraordinary implications for all of us in this philosophy. If the Creator is in all things, then the Creator's presence is in each of us and surrounds us every second of every day! We are never alone! We can go into the fields and woods, as I have done over the course of my entire life, knowing that the trees and the grass and every creature we see, and the rocks, the air, the rain, the snow, and even every snowflake, has part of the Creator in it! We are literally surrounded and engulfed by the Creator! We are as one with all Creation, and all Creation is as one with us! We are all related! We are all family! What a deep feeling of belonging this is!

One of a number of wonderful reminders of the Creator that northeastern Native Americans use every minute of every day is the band Kee's Ojibway people weave from twigs of their Grandmother Tree, the white cedar, plus yarrow and sweet grass; they wear it around their wrist or neck. In the daily lives of Ojibway people, this band is a constant reminder of the Creator. Sweet grass is said to produce good thoughts; yarrow is thought to ward off evil spirits; and white cedar is a healer, protector, and a gift of supreme importance from the Creator.

There are constant, daily reminders built into other northeastern American Indian faiths as well. For instance, Del Logan and the Onondaga people are reminded every waking moment of the Creator's Presence in their daily lives and of their role in all Creation. Actually, all people need reminders for we earthlings do temporarily forget this

Presence because we are human, and we are considered the lowest of God's creatures for this reason. We are the only beings in the universe that do not instinctively do what the Creator intends for us; we thus even needed an Emissary from the Creator (an Ojibway concept)—a first elder-teacher, as it were—to teach us how to live. Yet even with this gift of an instructor, we still stray too often from these teachings.

The first daily reminder for Onondaga people is a powerful one. Given that the Creator is in all things, the Creative Force empowers all things. Thus the ability of food to nourish them is the power of the Creator in their food. The power of pots and pans to hold their cooking food, of tables to put plates of food on, and of chairs to support them while they eat is the power of the Creator in these objects. The ability of clothes to warm them is the power of the Creator in the material from which their clothes are made, and the ability of dwellings to shelter them is the power of the Creator in the materials from which their homes are constructed.

Other examples of the constant daily reminder of the Creator's Presence among the Iroquois people involve ordinary activities. Since the Iroquois are human beings, they are brought up to believe they are fallible. The Great Spirit, the Creator of all Creation is, of course, the only infallible one. Thus when Del made a cornhusk doll, she could not put a face on it, for only the Creator can make a face; when she constructed any object, like a bowl, clothes, or a wampum belt, she had to put a mistake in it, for only the Creator is perfect; and when she wove a berry basket, as she did for our family, she had to leave open spaces in the weave pattern so that the Creator's Spirit in the collected berries could breathe and continue to live. Berries need air and space. Have you ever picked wild strawberries and filled a tin pail, only to arrive home and discover the fruit at the bottom of the pail had turned to mush and was ruined?

In addition to these sorts of daily reminders, there are other objects that take on Creator-inspired powers for a specific person or group of people. I have such an object, a large splint basket made for me when I was a child by Anna Escanaba, our Ojibway neighbor from the

Daily Reminders of the Creator's Many Gifts to Northeastern Indian People

settlement on Partridge Lake, Wisconsin. There is nothing pretentious or different about this basket's construction or appearance; it was made in the traditional way with traditional materials and natural dyes. But this basket has proved to be no ordinary basket. It has come to show special powers. Originally, it was a precious basket because Anna made it, and it accompanied me everywhere I lived: Star Lake and River Hills, Wisconsin; Fairfield, Southport, New Haven, and Washington, Connecticut; and Topsfield, Massachusetts. Then I had my Indian vision in 1970, and suddenly this basket took on a life force of its own. After that date the basket accompanied me on every lecture and every Indian Institute fundraising call I made, certainly in the hundreds and probably in the thousands after thirty-five years of use. The result? In the basket's presence, my fundraising was a phenomenal success considering how little I knew about it and how uncomfortable I felt doing it.

The basket also carries large numbers of Indian artifacts and appropriate books to share with interested people every time I feel it is important or I am asked to do so. I go so heavily laden at times that the basket is temporarily bent out of shape. It has been taken in and out of closets, in and out of cars, in and out of homes, and in and out of meeting places. It has been exposed to rain and sleet and snow, and has suffered through extremely hot and freezing temperatures as well. This basket is now sixty-eight years old, and yet, when a person looks at it today, except for the fact that the dyes on the outside are slightly faded, it still appears as if it were made yesterday. The sight of the basket gives me the confidence to pursue my dreams and the continued spiritual support of the Ojibway woman of my youth who made it. This basket, by the artifacts it has carried for eager viewers and by its meaning and presence to me, has helped me immeasurably to educate thousands of people of all ages and raise millions of dollars to benefit our Indian Institute. To me, this is the ultimate evidence of the Creator's Spirit in a specific object for a specific task to support and enhance a project that is "meant to be."

Basket Made by Anna Escanaba
and Given to Ned Swigart as a Boy

In addition to the Ojibway, Onondaga, and northeastern American Indian faith in the Creator that is so appealing and so convincing to me, and that forms the heart of my beliefs, there are several other key aspects of my own unique personal life— as there are in all our lives—which have reinforced, and still reinforce, my beliefs.

It was Del Logan and her Onondaga perspective that helped me work through a dilemma, which I shared with her during one of our precious opportunities to exchange our deepest thoughts. The story concerns my struggles during a period when, with the best of intentions, I wandered from my life-path. Early in my marriage to Debbie, I became actively involved in the Episcopal church that she served with such dedication, and subsequently, in the early 1960s, I was appointed lay-chaplain of the Gunnery School in Connecticut. I observed and took part in many different religious services representing very different religious approaches to life. During this time I became more and more confused by a personal dilemma that I believe many of us experience at some point in our lives. A number of the people who practiced these different faiths were led to believe that theirs, and theirs alone, was the true faith and represented the true God. How could this be? How could all these dedicated, faithful believers think theirs was the true God and theirs the true path to Heaven? And if they did, and if in fact there was only one right track, which one was it?

Therefore, it was a great relief for me to learn from Del of the way her faith and other northeastern American Indian faiths deal with this question of exclusivity and sectarian religion in a logical and positive way.

Del expressed her belief that every person must establish their own bond with the Great Spirit. To her, the life-journey of faith is like climbing a mountain to find the one Creator of us all and of our universe. Native Americans believe their faith is a personal and individual one, and that all people's journeys of faith must be equally respected. The "mountain" has many different trails for people of different religious persuasions to ascend, and all trails lead to the same peak and the same Presence.

It is true, I have not seen nor can I touch this Force, but perhaps someday we may have an understanding of what life and the Creative Force really are, or, on the other hand, we may never know. Is this of vital importance to me now? No. I am at peace with the inner knowledge that what I have felt and what I have seen again and again of a Creator's Presence, support, and encouragement in my life path has proven itself real to me.

Now, come walk with me to the next group of exhibits about our responsibilities here on Mother Earth. As we do, I must add a personal note.

Chapter 4

The Original Teachings of the Great Creator's Emissary

After the creation of the universe, including humans, was completed, the Creator realized that, of all the creatures of the Earth, human beings appeared to be the only ones in need of help to understand their role. The Creator thus sent down a Spiritual Emissary to the Anishinaabeg, "the people who came from the place beyond where the sun rises." This was the name the Ojibway people chose long ago to represent their Confederacy, made up, traditionally, of the Ojibway, Potawatomi, and Ottawa, and stretching from western Minnesota to Quebec. This Emissary was sent to teach the ways of the Creator and the Creation surrounding the Anishinaabeg and the sun-path or journey through life that the Anishinaabeg should try to follow.

This Emissary taught the elders of the Anishinaabeg, and they were instructed to teach the next generation of future elders. Thus, the elders become the keepers of the traditions for the Ojibway, responsible for passing on their faith and cultural heritage.

By way of introduction to the upcoming exhibits, let us think on this. As an example of what the Emissary and the elders have handed down from generation to generation, I want to share what Kee taught me about this from an Ojibway perspective:

> …there is no end, no end to anything or anyone, for the Sacred Shape given by the Creator is the Circle which has no end and continues on and on. This is not a difficult belief for people who live close to nature. They see that *nothing is lost*. The structure of bone becomes the structure of plants. The water of rain enters the life-blood of trees. Recycled by the land, biological waste becomes the nature of corn. Rabbit becomes coyote; fish becomes man; man becomes Mother Earth. The

red philosophy reasons that, if in the recycling not a cell of man's body is wasted, how much more then should it be that the most precious part of man, his very soul, should also not be wasted. The customary reference to life in this world is spoken of as "in this cycle," for the cycles of spirit continue on as do the cycles of matter — overlapping each other unto seven times seven times seven.

When, at any point in the unknown cycles a spirit is so qualified, it may enter the pool of the super blessed ones on the Blessed Isle [the Land of Souls, or Heaven]. That time of qualification is not known, nor does anyone pretend to know the qualifications for himself, nor to judge the spiritual qualification of another. It is enough responsibility for a human being, in his stage of development within this cycle, to maintain his material self with efficiency and his spiritual self with honor....

When a spirit enters the cycle of life on this earth what cycle of life he is on is not of importance here. What is important? That his feet be planted upon the sun-trail, the course between his own east, which leads, with the sun, to the west, and that this trail be walked with honor — to himself, to his family, to his clan, to his tribe, to his ancestors, to his descendants, to the Creator. This trail of life is the *Gissis-Mikana*.[3]

Notice a very important point Kee has made. The measure of a human being's success in life, is not which specific sun-path a person follows, but the direction they travel and how they go about walking the sun-path they have chosen. A person's sun-path is not preordained, as some people might think, but is left up to us to choose and to follow, employing in some way our unique life-gifts, that is, the abilities we have been given so that we may serve the Creator, Mother Earth, and our fellow human beings.

The role of elder-teachers is also treasured by the Onondaga people. They believe that the older people get, the wiser and more revered they become because of what they have experienced during their lifetime. Think for a moment about this very logical role of elderly people in a society and what this idea might mean in our present Western world.

Del Logan visited us often and taught us her people's Old Way of looking at the elderly in a modern context. The dedication she wrote to our eight-year-old son Paul in her book *Memories of Sweet Grass*, clearly illustrates the premise:

> Dedicated to Paul,
> My good friend who likes to read, hear stories of the past, loves nature. He also proved what my people have always believed, that there is never any generation gap.
>
> Paul fished, and I sat and watched him. He shot at his target with his bow and arrow.
>
> He brought me a chair to sit on each time I needed one. On my good days I would find a place to sit and watch him. But never did we feel that I was too old or he was too young, even though we are sixty years apart.
>
> We always said "thank you" when we finished our day.
> Sincerely,
> Del
> Washington, Connecticut
> 1977

Consider what a big difference this concept would make in our society, this belief among northeastern American Indians in the extraordinary value of elderly people as the purveyors of a nation's traditions to the next generation, and the respect and care for the elderly that this demands as a result.

Chapter 5

Father Sun, Mother Earth, Grandmother Moon, and the Stars of the Milky Way

Now that we have learned how the northeastern Native American people have viewed the Creator and the Creator's Emissary over their long history, we move on to the next exhibit, entitled "The Land." This exhibit presents the people's close association with Mother Earth. As we explore it, I would like to share, from my Ojibway heritage, a daily routine I follow of offering frequent prayers of thanksgiving for the gifts with which the Creator has blessed us. The nature of these prayers is similar to those offered by Iroquoian and other Algonquin Nations as well.

First, when I wake up in the morning I offer thanks to the Creator for the extraordinary gift of another day of life, for my angel wife by my side, for loving family and friends, and for all the potential challenges that the new day offers me.

I then offer thanks for Father Sun who is giving the light, warmth, life, and the new beginnings I am experiencing this day.

As I leave the house in the morning, I look down at our Mother Earth and give thanks for her gifts of healing, growth, renewal, and of solace for those of us whose loved ones have passed over and whom we miss as daily companions in this world, even though we believe we will see them upon occasion in the future.

Driving or walking to and from work, I am struck by the beautiful land that I pass, and I thank the Creator for our Big Sisters, the plants, and for our Big Brothers, the animals, for not only do they sustain me, but also I have learned so much from them.

As my day passes, I give thanks at appropriate times for my successes and my challenges—note, there are no "failures" in Native American thinking, only "challenges." I also give thanks for the many important resources in my life furnished by Mother Earth, such as my clothes and finally my shelter as I arrive home from my day of activities elsewhere to join my family.

As darkness approaches I give thanks to Grandmother Moon, who will look out for me and my family during the night.

And finally, when I go to bed, I review and give thanks for all the blessings of that day, and I pray for another fruitful day of service on the 'morrow, should it be the Creator's Will.

We have reached our second exhibit, so now let us turn our attention to the large role the land plays in Indian life as a whole.

Chief Big Eagle of the Golden Hill Paugussett Nation, who very recently passed over and whose portrait also watches over us from our Hall of Elders, uttered this profound comment in 1989: "Ours is a land culture. In fact, the land is the culture." Notice, therefore, that Native American identity is indivisible from Mother Earth. Let us read together about this exhibit from the Indian Institute brochure *The Land*:

> The Golden Hill Paugussetts, Pootatuck, Weantinock, and Schaghticoke, are Algonquin peoples who lived in western Connecticut. Their identities are all closely linked to specific places. Within each traditional homeland, there were dozens of settlements including isolated or paired wigwams, clusters of wigwams, and small villages. A sense of community—living together in a place—linked those who lived near one another.
>
> Here we share the land with ancestors, walking ground where our elders met and traditional ceremonies were held for centuries. Even if our jobs take us to new places, we still remember these connections. So did our ancestors when they moved away from the colonists to live with kin in other

communities or to build small farmsteads in nearby towns.

On Golden Hill near Trumbull, Connecticut, a one-quarter acre parcel is all that remains from the original reserve of 1659. Traditional leader Big Eagle, Aurelius Piper, lives where his ancestor Tom Sherman did at the end of the 18th century, surrounded by their people's lands.

Notice what such a relationship with the land could mean today. What a perfect counterbalance this life-view is to the Christian and Jewish Old Testament lesson (Genesis I, verse 28) that indeed involves a sense of stewardship, but with a caveat: "Replenish and subdue the earth and have dominion over every living thing." The traditional Indian relationship to Mother Earth is the reason Native American people over much of this country believe they can never own the land, even the land they live on. The land is the Great Spirit's Creation, the domain of Mother Earth. The Great Creator has designated human beings as stewards for their entire lives, free however only to use the land, care for it, and share it with all living creatures, including other human beings.

The different concepts of what stewardship means to white people of European extraction and traditional Indian people have resulted in many misunderstandings throughout history. When the white settlers first came and asked if they could live in an area, the Indians believed that they, as first comers, could not own the land but at least could share their home territory with these people. So the "rent" (a colonial term) for the settlers to share the land they occupied was small: a blanket or a pot, perhaps. Unfortunately, the white settlers—entering the negotiations with a western European tradition of ownership of the land, along with their feelings of cultural and religious superiority, and a misunderstanding of language—thought they were buying the land, and at a much-coveted bargain price, as well. When the Indians returned the following spring, as they believed to be their right, the settlers considered them to be trespassing illegally on land that they believed was now theirs alone. With language barriers and different cultural beliefs, serious disagreements such as this were bound to occur. This was not because Indians and whites initially hated one another; it was because, culturally, they had very different views concerning so many things, including religion and people's relationship with Mother Nature and all of Her bounty. Sadly for all concerned, the two groups too often did not realize or deal with these differences before problems arose.

Traditional northeastern American Indians also cannot own personal possessions, for these, too, are part of Mother Earth. In fact, the belief of the people of many Indian nations, including the Iroquois, is that the more a person treasures an item, the more a person is obligated to give that item, in love, to someone dear to them, such as Del's gifts to us and to our museum.

This brings up an important point concerning how our Western culture and the Algonquin-Iroquois Old Way differ in defining a successful life. In the context of what I have been taught about Ojibway, Onondaga, and other northeastern Native American beliefs, many aspects of Western culture—although they appear to be positive from the perspective of our culture's definition of success—can in fact be at odds with the whole reason for our existence: service. For example, Western culture puts a premium on earning enough money to buy the trappings of success: the proper home, clothes, clubs, schools, friends, places to vacation, careers, automobiles, and on and on. What a terrible waste of natural resources and what a poor system this is by which to judge a person's character and status. Notice these Western goals represent what traditional northeastern American Indians are cautioned to avoid at every opportunity. The Iroquois, for instance, are reminded by their crooked mask to beware of greed, conceit, and irresponsibility. To an Indian living in the traditional way, money, and what it can buy in these terms, is irrelevant. Rather, an Indian is taught to base their opinion of the social and personal worth of an individual on how they serve our Creator (or God), Mother Earth, their fellow human beings, and the people of their nation. If it is the Creator's Will that some money may come their way, they must use it as part of their life of service. This is what makes traditional Indian people, and those who believe in the Indian Way, truly "wealthy."

I cannot help but think, at this time, that Del is an example of a person who lived what she believed and thereby made a supreme sacrifice regarding her life-path at an early age. Del and her brother Alpheus both took an oath never to marry or have children. The world they knew from the perspective of their life on the Onondaga Reservation in Nedrow, New York, and the lives of their family before them was so cruel that they felt their life-paths were better directed toward trying to improve the lives of their Reservation brothers and sisters. Del had shared with us privately that she really loved children, as traditional Iroquois people do; but she was quick to add that this life with no children of her own was all right, for all of the people on the Nedrow "Rez," as she called it, were her "family," and all the children in the lower grades of the Syracuse school system where she taught were her children, as well. Apparently she also felt as deeply drawn to my close, warm, and welcoming family as we felt toward her in our need for her elder's wisdom and love. We became her family, and she became our grandmother figure. She would regularly arrive at our house with her car filled with gifts. Included, always, were a number of family treasures, such as her mother's Eel Clan spoon; the cradleboard she, her brother, and several generations of her ancestors had been strapped to as babies; her water drum; her brother's lacrosse stick and snow snake (a pole to throw competitively along an ice-covered trench in winter); her family's twig decoys; and a strawberry basket she herself had made long ago. We, in turn, passed these on to the Indian Institute in love. We felt strongly that these precious and sacred items should be cared for and protected so that many people in future generations could also see and learn from them. A number of Del's gifts are on exhibit in this museum, especially in the Indian Longhouse Classroom, which we will visit later.

As we now move to the next exhibit on our Big Sisters, the Plants, let us talk about a fourth aspect of our universe. Beside Grandfather Sun,

Mother Earth, and Grandmother Moon, there are the stars. To Ojibway elders, the stars of the Milky Way, which we can see on a clear night, are the campfires of human soul-spirits who have recently passed over and who are on a three- or four-day journey along the Path of Souls to the Land of Souls to the west. Each night for three or four nights Ojibway may go out, as I did after my father's passing over, and recognize the star that is the campfire of that loved one taking part in this journey; and after the completion of this journey a person can stop grieving and may then take part in the Feast of the Dead.

This Path of Souls through the Milky Way leads to a "bridge" over a river, the gateway to the Land of Souls, a higher level of existence. It is there that the Creator greets the soul-spirit of the person who has passed over. The Creator has a ledger of the life of the person who approaches the bridge. Recorded in this ledger are two columns: The first is a list of all the good things this person has done during their lifetime, and the second, all the acts that went against the Creator's will (all human beings are fallible). After a discussion of the merits of this list, if a person has done more good than bad deeds and has left the Earth a better place than they found it, that person will be allowed to pass over the bridge to join the circle of their ancestors in the Land of Souls.

But what if the ledger is not favorable for the person who has passed over, what if their bad deeds outnumber their good ones? I think the concept of "evil," of where bad things come from, can be one of the most interesting teachings of the Ojibway faith. A person who does more bad than good deeds is turned back from the bridge by the Creator, and their soul is damned to wander the Earth forever. "Badness" or "evil" is a type of aura emitted by the soul-spirits of those who have passed over but whose lives have not been worthy of admission to the Land of Souls. In addition to the Aura of the Creator and the aura created by people of good will, this bad aura also surrounds us. We must be very careful to keep focused on the Creator and all the forces for good in our world. If, instead, we let our guard down for even a moment, which we all are prone to do on occasion, we may be drawn into doing bad acts by the bad aura that may encompass us at that moment. The inevitable result is that nice people can do bad things, sometimes without even knowing it. You have all heard about and undoubtedly done this yourself. We have a saying in our Western world that "the road to hell is paved with good intentions."

I can honestly say that during my seventy-eight years, I have never known someone well whom I would say was a "bad" person as defined by the Ojibway explanation. I have seen, however, basically decent people do hurtful, even evil things, including myself, as unintentional as it might have been. To me, the Ojibway concept of evil, therefore, is a satisfying explanation of why, after a bad day at work, I would say or do something hurtful to someone I loved when I got home, a person who was blameless in this situation; or why I think I'm really doing or saying the right thing, but to another person it is the worst possible choice of action or words.

This defines the parameters of good and bad (evil) for me in a way that is practical and real, that I can try to be aware of every day, and that I am able to do something about. This idea of a "ledger" kept by the Creator, no matter how farfetched it may seem, is of great comfort to me in its essential and most fundamental challenge. To me it means we have within our own lifetime the opportunity to make sure we serve the Creator and all Creation every day of our lives in such a way that our good deeds will outnumber the bad deeds that we try to avoid but that we end up doing anyway, knowingly or unknowingly, as the imperfect beings we know that we are.

Chapter 6

How Ojibway People View the World around Them: The Plants and the Animals

The next two exhibits are about the Algonquin and Iroquois relationship with their Big Sisters, the plants, and their Big Brothers, the animals. We are now at the exhibit on plants.

In the teachings handed down by the Creator's original human Emissary and later by generations of Ojibway elder-teachers, plants are considered the highest form of life because they are independent of all living creatures. All they need is sunlight, air, and water to survive. Since plants occupy this position, the Ojibway and other Algonquin and Iroquois people must treat them with utmost respect and address them as "Big Sister."

According to Del Logan, corn, our exhibit subject, is spoken of by Iroquois people in their Creation story and is described as having sprung from the grave of Sky Woman, who died giving birth to twin boys, Good Minded and Bad Minded. It was the milk in the corn that nourished them. According to Del, "Corn was the greatest gift of the Creator to the American Indian. The knowledge of corn as a crop, which not only provided daily food but could also be stockpiled for the future, meant independence from hunting and resulted in the establishment of more permanent [and larger] communities. Among the agriculturalists of the Eastern Woodland Indians, corn became, in life and legend, THE life sustainer."[4]

In addition, the corn plant was a greater source of nourishment than all of the other cultivated food plants combined and as such dominated Iroquoian and other Northeastern American Indian food getting and ceremonial activities. Also, once harvested corn could be stored for long periods of time without spoiling and could be used in myriad ways—enjoyed fresh from the field uncooked, or boiled, roasted, parched, dried and ground into meal, and mixed with dried nuts, berries, or meat. Other parts of this plant were used as well. The husks were employed for insulation or coverings for Indian dwellings, and braided into mats for sleeping. The cobs were used as pipes for smoking, scrubbers for washing clothes, and for other purposes.

Corn is also an example of the importance of plants as a provider of large, dependable food reserves. Domesticated plants such as corn were a major factor in the stability of the living conditions of the Iroquois Confederacy and pre-colonial Algonquin Indians wherever it was warm enough for these plants to grow. Traditional northeastern American Indians recognized the great importance of plants in the following way: If a human being was going to harvest a plant for food, medicinal, or technological purposes, the Ojibway and Onondaga people practiced a ritual that involved approaching the plant-spirits and offering a prayer of apology to the Creator's Spirit in the first plant of the species they were going to harvest, saying: "I am sorry, Big Sister, that I must take your life, but I too must live." This first plant is then left untouched to inform the others, and the harvesting may begin. In respect for this Big Sister and the Creator's Life-Spirit within it, harvested plants had to be treated at all times with respect, as in the example I mentioned earlier about placing berries in a container that allows them to breathe. This approach has been used by northeastern American Indians for hundreds and perhaps thousands of years.

In addition to domesticated plants like the Three Sisters corn, beans, and squash, there are many other wild plants that are equally important. The first group is classified as non-woody-stemmed plants, but to an Indian botanist like Kee, they are simply everything but trees and shrubs. The two examples I wish to share are the cattail and the milkweed. When fresh-water cattail is harvested, the shoots are used as food; the leaves are saved for weaving mats; the typical brown seed cylinder on top of the leafless stem, when rolled in evergreen sap, is employed as a torch at night; the down from the seed pods, if ripe, is used as an insulating material for blankets and clothes; and the roots are dried and ground (they are very stringy otherwise) as a starch and made into a potato pancake–like dish.

In the case of milkweed, the stem fibers are woven into string for bows and other uses; and the shoots, flowers, and fruit (while it is still white inside) are used for food.

Woody-stemmed plants—trees and shrubs, Kee called them—are the second group of plants. Two good examples are the white oak and the white pine. The white oak is a beautiful shade tree with strong wood that can be used for tools or tool handles, or for firewood and other crafts. This oak also has an inner bark, which, when made into a poultice, is extremely effective in preventing human wounds from getting infected and even in curing infections that have already occurred. The acorn (nut) can be stored for the winter and used for food. White oak acorns are gathered in the fall and are boiled or roasted to remove as much tannic acid as possible. The nuts then can be ground into a powdery substance and used as the cattail roots are.

The white pine is also an extraordinarily useful tree and is venerated by some nations, such as the Iroquois Confederacy, which believes it to be a "Tree of Peace," a symbol of the life and strength of their Confederacy. The small dead twigs and limbs of white pine are very combustible, even when wet, and like white birch bark, when a spark is added, make the beginnings of an excellent fire. The green cambium between the bark and the wood is nutritious and can be eaten in winter, giving rise to the word "Adirondacks" or "bark eaters" used by the Iroquois to refer to the Algonquin people around them. Best of all, when crushed and put into boiling water, the green needles of this evergreen tree make a flavorful drink containing vitamin C. This drink was used by northeastern American Indian people to ward off what the Western world knew as the terrible wasting disease that first attacks the gums of the mouth and was later called "scurvy."

There is a famous story about French explorer Jacques Cartier and his expedition. They became trapped by winter ice in the St. Lawrence River in 1635. Running out of fresh fruit and vegetables, many of the men came down with the symptoms of scurvy. The surviving expedition members were eventually treated by local Algonquin Indians, who showed them how to make the evergreen needle tea that provided the over-wintering Frenchmen with the vitamin C they needed. Most of those who were sick recovered within a short period of time, and they all continued to use this tea until spring when they were able to renew their journey.

Let us now move on to the exhibit on the deer. According to the teachings handed down by the Creator's original Emissary and later by generations of Ojibway elder-teachers, animals other than humans are considered to be the second highest form of life. This is because even though animals depend on plants and other animals for food, they always faithfully fulfill the Creator's role for them on Mother Earth. Since animals occupy this position, the Ojibway and other northeastern Algonquin and Iroquois people must treat them with utmost respect and address them as Big Brother.

According to Keewaydinoquay and Del Logan, the deer, our exhibit subject, is probably the most important animal resource in the northeast. As with corn, the deer is a supreme gift from the Creator to the American Indian. The deer itself not only provides food and has many other uses, but it also plays a major part in the political and social organization of nations. Algonquin and Iroquoian people list the deer and several other animals to represent the Providers, one of the five major political units that must exist to comprise a band, the smallest self-governing unit of a nation. All people who grow, harvest, and hunt food belong to the Providers.

Also, as with plants, when a Big Brother is killed, out of respect for the spirit of the animal and the Spirit of the Creator in the animal, human beings must use as many of its parts as possible. For instance, when the deer in this exhibit is killed, all available meat, including most of the internal organs, is used as food, either eaten fresh or preserved for later use by smoking or by freezing when the weather permits. The hide is prepared for making clothes and other household items;

ligaments and tendons are made into string-like cords for such items as bow strings; bones are used for many kinds of tools, including for chipping stone artifacts; bone marrow is extracted for food; the hooves are used in games and ground for glue.

Therefore, traditional northeastern American Indians recognize the great importance of animals with a practice similar to the one they use for plants. If a human being must kill an animal for food or other purposes, a prayer of apology must be offered to the Creator's Spirit and to the animal's spirit occupying the physical body of the animal: "I am sorry, Big Brother, that I must take your life, but I too must live."

Just think of the Western world's treatment of our Big Brothers to this day. Bird species, like the crow and sea ducks, are shot largely for sport; plumed birds are still killed for their feathers; and big game animals are still shot for a trophy head to mount on a wall. Think of all the fur-bearing animals trapped only for their hides, like the mink, the muskrat, and the beaver in the United States and Canada. Think of the buffalo, when they covered the plains—they were shot for sport from moving trains and left to rot, or killed only for their tongue or hide, the rest left for the buzzards to eat. One does not treat a Big Brother in this way.

I think often of when the English, French, and Dutch first introduced commercial trapping in early colonial times to nations like the Ojibway, the Onondaga, and other northeastern American Indian groups, whose cultures taught them of the virtue of treating these Big Brothers with great respect. Indian trappers were paid by the colonists to kill mammals for their skins alone for the European clothes and hat markets. In return the Indians were given credit at the trading posts to purchase the white man's goods to make their lives arguably more comfortable. But what a cultural price Indian trappers must have paid! In killing mammals only for their skins and being increasingly unable themselves to utilize as fully as possible the remainder of the animals, as their Indian faith demanded, the trappers had to turn away from an important aspect of their relationship to their Big Brothers. One can see how this and other white-induced changes began, from the very start, to strain the whole fabric of Native American political-religious-social beliefs.

As we look at the exhibits about the plants and the animals, you may be wondering where human beings belong in the hierarchy of life.

When I was active in the Christian Church, I was taught that human beings are the highest form of life and have been given by God the freedom to make day-to-day decisions regarding our life-path. However, from my experience seeing, reading about, and studying human history and behavior, I have become increasingly aware of the tendency of human beings throughout history to choose knowingly or unknowingly the path of bad over good; to ravish and destroy our environment rather than serving as stewards for it; and to kill, torture, starve, and subjugate our fellow human beings, often for no better reason than selfish social, economic, political, or religious concerns. Many recent examples illustrating man's inhumanity to man come to mind: Hitler and the Jewish people; the Catholic-Protestant fighting in Northern Ireland; the Serbian, Croatian, and Bosnian ethnic warfare; the Arab-Israeli conflict; and the African sectarian tribal wars. Given this obvious human tendency to choose evil, how can we be the highest form of life, second only to God? It did not make any sense to me then, and it does not make any sense to me now.

However, the message shared by northeastern American Indian elder-teachers does make sense. Because humans do not always follow the lessons of their Big Sisters, the plants, and their Big Brothers, the animals, who live their lives as the Creator intended, humans are the least of God's creatures. Worse yet, we do not even follow the examples of fellow human beings who have envisioned and have contributed to a world of understanding and peace over the centuries. In fact, during their lifetimes we have persecuted and even killed these visionaries—such figures as Christ, Gandhi, and Martin Luther King, Jr., immediately come to mind.

The religious, social, and political applications that arise from the northeastern Indian's hierarchy of life forms not only make sense to me but also involve constant reminders of the Creator's role in our daily lives.

Let us move on to the next exhibit now, and while we do, let us explore the Indian system of government.

Chapter 7

A System of Government

The form of government that traditional northeastern American Indian nations practiced and, wherever and whenever possible, still utilize, has been influenced by their Big Brothers, the animals. First, animals serve as teachers for humans to emulate in hunting, fishing, and individual and group behavior. They become role models for human beings to follow in serving the Creator and their nations. Secondly, animal duties and their social order in the natural world serve as examples for the political system of northeastern American Indians.

I too have learned many lessons from my animal-friends over the years. I would like to share a few of these with you.

A wise elder-teacher, Phillip Deer of the Muskogee people, once told me that when ducks and geese fly no one has to tell them which direction is north or south. And a hawk sitting in a tree does not join them—he remains a hawk. I asked myself, could we do that? Do we know as clearly who we are, instinct-wise, and what we are meant to do, behavior-wise, during our days on this Earth? The animals have much to teach us: the cooperation and necessary stamina of wolves running down a deer; the cleverness of a red fox to head off a gray squirrel from escape until it becomes confused—an easy pounce for the fox; and the stealth of a bobcat, motionless and crouching in the woods as an unsuspecting gray squirrel approaches just close enough. I have learned from the sacrifice of animal-mothers caring for their young: a doe rearing, legs flailing, when I got too close to her fawn with my camera; and a mother grouse puffing up her feathers and running right at my younger son on a woodland trail, and then pretending she had a broken wing to give her half-grown babies a chance to run and hide. I have learned of love as a male cardinal gently feeds his mate in a bush before the young are born; of the responsibilities of parenthood, as yet another male cardinal feeds the young which, having left the nest, are still learning how to fend for themselves while the cardinal's mate is busy with having a second family; and of the role of older children who help raise their younger siblings, as young bluebirds from the first nesting help their mother and father raise a third brood. After a fresh light snowfall of three consecutive days, my son and I observed the tracks of an undersized, late fawn of the year about to be run down by a coyote, and a large adult deer coming to its rescue. The adult deer leapt right at the coyote and led it on a frantic two-mile chase until the coyote gave up, then the adult returned to the exhausted fawn, who followed it and at night bedded down against its side until the story ended with the melting snow three days later.

The northeastern and other Indian people have a tradition involving a relationship and understanding between a human being and a specific bird or animal species, and there is one species of animal that has come to occupy a very special place in my family's life; this animal has become my totem, my guardian-spirit-teacher, a gift from the Creator. This animal is the wolf. As often as I can, I carry in my pocket a wolf fetish that has been smudged (purified) and blessed by my Tlingit friend, Ed Sarabia. This talisman reminds me, as I feel its presence, of the attributes of this animal: faithfulness, loyalty, and the surrender of self for the good of the family group. A wild pack of wolves used to accompany my father when he went bird hunting in northern Wisconsin, and would come out and sit with him when he stopped for lunch—as impossible as that may sound to a person unfamiliar with this tradition. Dad even fed them chocolate bars.

I also have had extraordinary experiences with wolves. The most dramatic of these took place some fifteen years ago at our rural Connecticut home. My wife came rushing in one day from her early morning walk with our dog. She breathlessly related that they had seen a large doe lying dead on our pond's sandy beach, perhaps sixty feet from our back porch. I hastened out to see what I could learn. Immediately I noticed that the deer had been killed in the special wolf way, not by nipping at the entire animal, as packs of wild dogs and even coyotes will, but by tearing at the hamstrings of the lower legs, ripping at the neck, and then immediately beginning to eat the animal, particularly in the belly area.

My first impression was that this just wasn't possible. To my knowledge there had been no wolves "recorded" in many years in Connecticut, but then I had been told not too many years earlier that there had been no black bears officially recorded either when I saw evidence of a bear tipping over and spreading the contents of our Indian Institute dumpster all over the nearby woods. According to state police and state biologists, "it was probably the work of teenage pranksters." But in a year or two, several bears were seen by a number of people in the immediate area, and bears then became officially recorded as present in this area of Connecticut. Could this be another such case?

I had hardly finished these thoughts when out of the corner of my eye I saw a huge wolf appear, as if by magic, from the adjoining woods. I immediately recognized him as a wolf from my Wisconsin days. He was probably an alpha wolf (pack leader) given his size—approximately six feet in length; his coat was gray and brown, and he had a German Shepard-like shape but with a longer snout, narrower front chest, and front legs that were very close together. The wolf approached me and then sat down no more than seven feet away, also looking at the doe— to share this victory, perhaps? He was dignified and alert, but appeared to be as friendly as any pet dog, just the way wilderness wolves used to behave with my father and me over fifty years before in Wisconsin. I felt no fear. This was my totem, my guardian-spirit-teacher, here to remind me of the bond that we had had so many years ago that, like my faith, was still an all important part of me. I talked to him as I had to the wild wolves my family knew so long ago and so far away, welcoming him and telling him with hand gestures and a gentle voice that I would get help and pull the doe into the woods on the other side of the pond for him and his pack to eat. He cocked his head in a familiar fashion as though carefully listening to my words, which of course people will say was impossible, and then he got up and slowly wandered away up the dam, pausing periodically to look back at me.

I called a friend who came over and helped me drag the deer over the dam and into the woods to return the pack's prey to its rightful owners. When I came back the next day to see what had happened, I found the animal had been essentially stripped of meat.

Of course, I called the proper state officials right away. I explained everything -- growing up with wolves in northeastern Wisconsin; our special family relationship with them; the size, color, and body characteristics of the one I had seen; and the relatively unique method of killing its prey. Despite all of this corroborating evidence, I was firmly told that there were no verified wolf sightings in Connecticut.

I have not seen the alpha wolf again. Did he and his pack find it too densely settled here, needing, as they do, such an immense, essentially wilderness-like territory upon which to hunt? Where did they go? I heard nothing further about them. Were there any other "verifiable" sightings? Did they move back north through the same wild corridor from Canada to northwestern Connecticut that bear and moose presumably take coming south, and that the wolf pack could have used to get here? Wolves seen and recorded in Massachusetts fairly recently speak to their presence in the region.

Think a moment on this meeting of mine with this pack of wolves. Think a moment, as I have, about the import of this event and the concept of a totem animal in the wild kingdom for each human being, an animal that provides human beings with a guardian-spirit-teacher. Think of this extraordinary bond between a human being and a species of wild animal that is feared by many, but that has held firm during our family's life in northeastern Wisconsin and still existed some fifty years later when this subsequent meeting between the alpha wolf and me occurred. Vast distances and many generations of wolves, perhaps with no close genetic ties to the Wisconsin animals, separated these contacts between the wolves and me, and yet the bond remains. Is this miraculous? Not really. For traditional Native American people, a special animal-person relationship is well known and accepted as a gift from the Creator.

Then there is still another category of experience that can and does occur—those unexplainable and almost mystical events that generate a sense of oneness between a human being and a Big Brother. For all-too-brief moments in time, there is a bond in which a human is not feared but trusted. I have so many personal examples and will share only a very few now: A young gray squirrel with a broken hind leg crawled up to me, a young boy, in the woods as if asking me for help, which I gladly gave, setting its leg and later releasing it; a mother black bear appeared suddenly on a precipitous mountain trail, waited only six feet away while her two cubs played around my feet until they tired of the game and returned to her, and then turned and went back the way she had come; and a three-quarters grown fawn came up to my wife and me on a woodland trail, bleating for its lost mother, which we helped her try to find. Finally, there's the case of the supreme loyalty and trust of a pet, and the view of some people that animals have no afterlife: Our precious pet kitten, shot and paralyzed in the hindquarters by an undisciplined hunter, able to use only her front paws, crawled back to our garage from God knows how far. Appearing to be in terrible pain, she stared up at us then settled down immediately in my wife's arms, at peace there, and later dying there, peacefully. Heartbroken, we shared with our minister in Topsfield, Massachusetts, our grief and our hope that we would see our beloved kitten again. In an amazingly insensitive way, he referred to the Scriptures, saying that we would not see our cat again because no animal, other than a human being, had a soul, could reason, or could go to Heaven. This was dogma at its worst, with no human emotion, and it did not—and does not—sit well with us.

Historically, such an idea is nonsensical to people of northeastern American Indian faith, for their Big Brothers, the animals, have a soul-spirit equal to our own. Thus, in the cycle of life, they will be with us every step of the way. How comforting this is to those of us who have known an animal's love and companionship.

Among all of the contributions which animals have given northeastern Native Americans, one stands out for its far reaching effect on the entire structure of Indian society: It is the role of animals in the Indian political system. As far back as the oral tradition exists, northeastern nations have been politically and socially organized according to a clan system. A clan is identified by its members' descent from a common human ancestor. Clans traditionally represent one of five different social roles and are named after appropriate animal role models for these activities. To this day representatives of the five clans are needed to comprise a band. A person is "born to" a clan, the clan of the father, or, in a few societies, like the Iroquois, the clan of the mother. However, a person may also switch clans, or be adopted by another clan because of special relationships to that clan or because of personal abilities that personify that clan's duties. Different nations may use different examples of what they think are the best animal role models, but the duties they represent are the same. The five social clan roles, as represented by various appropriate animals, are:

1) Leader—If a member of the Ojibway, for instance, belongs to the Crane, the Hawk, or the Eagle Clan, they are expected to be a Leader who serves the best interests of the nation at the expense of personal considerations.

2) Provider—Members of the Beaver, Moose, Caribou, and Deer Clans are the Providers. People serving in these clans are the hunters, farmers, fisherman, and arrow makers; they provide the material things the community needs, such as food, weapons, tools, and implements.

3) Defender—The Defenders' duty is to protect and guard the nation from any danger, such as enemy warriors, dangerous animals, or natural catastrophes. These clans are named after the bear, the wolf, and the lynx—all predators of other animals.

4) Teacher—The reasoning behind the animals chosen to represent the Teachers—the carp, the white fish, and the sturgeon—is typical of Indian logic. These fish lie very still at the bottom of deep pools of water, and they look up and quietly watch everything that goes on in the world above them.

5) Healer—For as long as Ojibway oral tradition has existed, Healers have been the doctors of mind and body, while many Western doctors are only recently learning and practicing this holistic approach. Healers belong mostly to the Otter and the Turtle Clans. A chosen few of these healers, like Keewaydinoquay, become members of a secret medicine society, the Midewewin, one of the oldest, most important, and most powerful of Ojibway societies. It is they who conduct all manner of human cures, including truly miraculous ones, examples of which I will soon share with you.

As for the Iroquois Confederacy, their form of government was so well conceived that during early colonial times Benjamin Franklin, Thomas Jefferson, and other politicians found the Iroquois doctrine of federalism and the Indian rules of governing valuable to the process of forming a new government for the former British colonies.

Thus it was that in framing the original Constitution and Bill of Rights for this country, these men borrowed heavily from the document drawn up by Hiawatha and Deganwidah (sometime before 1450) in forming the Iroquois Confederacy of five, and later six, nations: the Mohawk, Oneida, Onondaga, Cayuga, Seneca, and later, the Tuscarora. The Iroquois Nations call this document the "Great Law of Peace."

Each individual nation (in the United States Constitution, each colony and later each state) ruled its own territory, and its duly elected council (our state legislature) decided all issues of public policy concerning their nation and their nation only. In addition, a Grand Council comprised of all of the sachems of their allied nations (our elected representatives and senators from our fifty states) was held at least every five years in the fall at the central fire of the Onondaga (Washington, DC, in our case) to discuss all issues that involved the entire confederacy. These decisions became the law to be applied to all the nations equally (laws passed by the United States legislature). Each sachem had equal authority (one person, one vote), and how powerful he became was solely dependent on his oratorical abilities (not where he came from, how long he had been there, or the party and interest groups he represented). One sachem was allowed to speak at a time; civilian and military duties were separated; and the purpose of these meetings was aimed at educating and persuading (not confronting and intimidating). I might add that adhering to these rules is not always the case today in Indian governments either, for Iroquois life has been so influenced, knowingly or unknowingly, by ours over these last 300 years that they now also find much to argue about.

You have probably heard the words "matrilineal" and "patrilineal," and "matriarchal" and "patriarchal" used to describe how a nation is ruled. The Iroquois, for example, are matrilineal, meaning descent and clan membership are traced through the mother's line; whereas the Ojibway people and other northeastern Algonquin nations are patrilineal, or descend through the father's line. In true patriarchies, like the Ojibway and other northeastern nations, it is men, not women, who have control and power.

The Iroquois are matriarchal, but not quite fully so, even though their system gives women many important political and social responsibilities. Except in truly extraordinary situations, it does not give them ultimate control, which is held by a male chief. A woman's brother (if she has one), not the woman herself, has authority over her; but the brother does not have complete power either. In the Iroquois matrilineal system, even if the brothers of women are the supposed leaders, women do wield a lot of power, and this has resulted in an interesting system of checks and balances at the highest levels of Iroquoian government. It all has to do with the clan system. The women of each village's various clans elect a clan mother or leader. These clan mothers become part of a female council that, among other important duties, is responsible for the election of a new chief when necessary and can convene a hearing about an existing chief whose actions are being challenged by another member of their nation.

See this hat on display that Del made for me and that I gave to the Indian Institute? It is an Onondaga chief's hat. Notice that this hat has two fork-buck antlers (one branch or tine on each deer antler) attached to the sides. See how they wiggle? They are sewed on loosely, so if a person has a real grievance against the chief, he can come up and yank it off, and then the chief has to explain himself to the women's council of clan mothers.

Let me give you an example of how the Onondaga pick a chief and the means by which they judge him. As Del and I were driving by some of the bigger houses in Washington, Connecticut, on one of her first visits to us, Del grew unusually silent. After we had arrived at our home and had sat down at our kitchen table, Del pulled a picture of a house out of her handbag and gave it to me without a word. It was a small, single-story dwelling, badly in need of repair and a coat of paint. The yard was mostly dirt. The porch was sagging, and the front window was broken and patched with tape.

Then she spoke. "If the people you know saw this house in their neighborhood or on their street," she asked me, "what would they say about the family who lived in it?"

My answer was, "Not much."

She pursued the subject as she always did when she was about to make an important point. She said, "Some people in your town wouldn't like the appearance of this house, especially if it was nearby. They would be afraid it would reflect on them, afraid it would hurt the value of the neighborhood. They would say people who lived in that shack were lazy and shiftless." Then she went on to explain how a man was elected a chief of her people. The man who lived in this place was from an Iroquois reservation and was highly respected by the community. He could be a future chief, because he had the reputation of being a dedicated servant to his people during his entire lifetime. He had a college degree and a good job, but now he was using every penny he earned beyond his immediate and simple needs to help other reservation children attend schools and colleges and bring their skills back to their people.

Let us think for a moment about this traditional system of electing a chief. The most able women—those elected as clan mothers because of their dedication to their clan, their nation, and their people—can elect or reject a chief. Only the most able men are elected to serve because they have already proven themselves in terms of the highest standards of their nation: as stewards of their people and their world. This is one section from the Iroquois Great Law of Peace that our founding fathers did not use in the Constitution because of how they felt about women having a leadership role at that time; this problem still exists today. Women make up more than fifty percent of the population of the United States. Yet what is the percentage of women in the Senate or the House of Representatives, or as governors or in other areas of political responsibility in our country? It is significantly lower than the percentage of men.

In addition to electing chiefs, Onondaga women also ruled their households, controlled the use of their land, and provided probably three-quarters of the food their people ate. Men were the leaders, hunters and fishermen, and defenders. Notice men's and women's different but equally respected duties under the Iroquois system of rule.

If a nation within the Iroquois Confederacy had a serious disagreement with a nation outside the Confederacy, a Grand Council of the senior men from each Iroquois nation would be called to discuss it at length, for this was a grave problem for all. Everyone would have his turn to be heard. If war was finally considered the only option, then the chief, as the supreme leader of all the Iroquois nations, was expected to lead his warriors into action, and as many Council members as possible were to take part. I wonder how many military actions we would have today if the founding fathers and subsequent rulers of the United States and other nations personally led their men (and women) into battle as the Iroquois did. Or, if women leaders were responsible for electing a chief (the president), would they—as mothers—pick a president who would only go to war in the case of a true national emergency? In this way they would know their children would not be sent off to fight, and perhaps to die needlessly, in religious, economic, or politically motivated wars, as so many of our current global engagements appear to be today.

Regarding the youth who by default are sent to fight these engagements, they too often pay with their young lives. Who knows what humanity loses with each young death, what unique and valuable talent or service may be lost forever.

The second form of northeastern American Indian rule is the Algonquin people's patrilineal and patriarchal society. The male-oriented Algonquian family structure resembles that of generations of families in America, a structure which has relatively recently been changing through the efforts of women's advocacy groups and the trend toward equal opportunity. Unlike Del's Iroquoian people, Algonquin nations in pre-colonial times were living in more separated and smaller groups. This is because the Iroquois people migrated from the west and south into the area they later occupied: the five finger lakes of central New York State. Because of the moderating effect of the lake waters on the climate around the lakes, the Iroquois had a long enough growing season between frosts to raise species of corn, beans, and squash. With such a stable food supply they could live in larger settlements. Many of the Algonquian nations, on the other hand, living to the east, north, and west of the Iroquois, had no such moderating climatic conditions, and the frost-free time was too short to grow these domesticated crops. With less food to depend on and harsher weather conditions, the Algonquin nations were limited to smaller villages in summer and very small, extended-family settlements during the harsh winters. Because of this, the Algonquin political structure and the power of nation-groupings were more flexible than the Iroquois, and there were frequent power plays (like there are today in our world) around which Algonquian people's confederacies rose and fell. The result was a lineage situation in which women gained control of a nation, ostensibly through the patriarchal order of inheritance: chief, eldest son, eldest daughter's son, eldest daughter. Therefore, unlike their Iroquoian neighbors, whose women had political power but elected a male chief, within the Algonquin patriarchal society women were allowed to rule. There are records, far from complete, of women serving as leaders, including Aw-shucks, Chief of the Sakkonet, a member of the Wampanoag Confederacy; and Shaumpishuh, Chief of the Menunkatuck, a band of the Quinnipiacs.

According to Trudie Lamb Richmond:

> It is important to realize that women lived differently
> from tribe to tribe, and within tribes as individuals. For
> the most part sex roles were clearly defined and no one
> believed the other to be more or less demeaning. Each
> depended upon the other to fulfill his or her task—
> otherwise all suffered. The division of labor was little
> understood by the non-Indian. While women were the
> horticulturists, men were the hunters; while women
> preserved and prepared the food, men were the
> toolmakers; while women built the homes and cared for
> the family, the men protected them. Whatever the role,
> it was an essential one....One has to keep in mind that
> Indian women often knew from the time they were
> quite young what their role would be and what was
> expected of them. Yet women could and did occupy
> roles generally filled by the men, such as healers,
> herbalists, shamans, and chiefs.
>
> Unfortunately, there are some misconceptions
> surrounding descriptions of traditional women. Too
> often they have been depicted as beasts of burdens,
> drudges, slaves. Even the term "squaw," the Algonquin
> word for woman, evolved into a derogatory statement,
> prompted by the bias of European settlers and fur
> traders (who did not understand or respect our
> customs).
>
> Obviously what we are experiencing...is an attempt
> of one culture (yours) to apply its mores to another
> without attempting to understand the social structure
> and framework of a totally different way of life.[5]

Chapter 8

The Role of Humans

We have now completed our tour of the main exhibit hall. Come walk with me around the corner to our next stop, our large longhouse classroom, which illustrates the northeastern American Indians way of living as an integrated part of Mother Earth and how this Indian life-way applies to us today.

As we walk, I will introduce you to the role of Native Americans that we are about to explore in the longhouse. According to the Ojibway, in spite of the human position as the lowest form of life in the natural world, we have important roles to fulfill during our lifetime. The first, as I have previously mentioned, is the responsibility of serving the Creator as stewards of Mother Earth and our fellow human beings. Secondly, we are to serve the Creator in the very best way that we can all of our lives. To do this the Creator has given us two additional gifts: a unique talent and an ability to communicate with fellow human beings, with animals, and perhaps even with plants.

Ojibway and others believe that the Creator gives every human being a unique talent that will never be duplicated. Therefore, we are on a life-long quest to find this gift, and then to use it to the best of our ability to serve the Creator in a singular way. The process of self-discovery can take place at any time for women, but for men it usually begins at puberty with a vision quest. When, in the Creator's "eyes," an Ojibway has completed their sun-path, whether they are aware of this or not, their soul-spirit leaves this Earth for a higher level of existence.

The long-held Indian concept of the uniqueness of an individual has now been proved by modern science. Each human being is in fact born with a unique genetic inheritance, never to be duplicated in the natural world (notice, I use the words "natural world" because of the recent scientifically engineered system of cloning, which may or may not affect this concept). Because of this unique genetic inheritance, each person can potentially do something different and better than anyone else on Earth at any time. If a person searches diligently for, and then is receptive to this talent and what it may demand of them, they will probably discover it. However, in a significant number of cases this uniqueness may never be discovered by the individual, but from the time of their existence in the human uterus up to the time they are freed by the Creator from Mother Earth, their life-destiny will be fulfilled nonetheless according to the Creator's Will.

Think of what this could mean. A human being could be a miscarriage, stillborn, a month old, a year old, ten years old, fifty years old, a hundred years old—age is not a factor. The Creator will allow us to pass over only when we have completed our mission on Earth, whether or not we and those left behind are aware of it. This is a most comforting idea. For instance, it is particularly difficult to accept the passing over of a child late in a pregnancy or in infancy. My wife and I have experienced the former on five occasions. If you hold to the Ojibway philosophy, you believe that a child, no matter how old, has passed over to a higher level of being, having completed their reason for existence according to the Creator's view, despite what our limited perspective tells us. While at first this logic was clouded by our grief, over time it became increasingly clear to Debbie and me that these children lived and passed over so that, as their life purpose, we might offer a loving environment to other children already born who needed this support. And so it was. In addition to being the birth parents of three lovely children of our own—Lucie, Ted, and Paul—five additional children came into our lives. Also, during the twenty-three years I was a teacher in boarding school, my wife and I had many young people come to us seeking a family like ours for a variety of reasons. They have passed through our lives, and we continue to this day to offer what we can to each new generation of young and not-so-young people who wish to be a part of our family circle. It gives us great joy to be able to serve the Creator in this fashion.

Regarding this phenomenon of miraculous good arising from the ashes of profound earthly tragedy, I am reminded of an event shared with me a number of years ago. The narrative concerned two young girls dying of leukemia in the same room in a Boston, Massachusetts, hospital. Both had received the last rites. Only then was a group being trained in the healing ministry by Agnes Sanford, the wife of an Episcopal minister, called in to try to help the two girls. This small group went to the hospital. Neither child was expected to survive the night. While at the hospital, the group had been informed that one of the girls was the only remaining child of a mother who stayed with her every moment she could, and had recently lost both her husband and her only other child, a son, in an automobile accident.

The call finally came from the head doctor. One of the little girls was in remission and was now expected to recover. The other had died peacefully in her sleep, free of pain and further suffering, and the mother was with her deceased daughter as he spoke. The group returned to the hospital to see, and, hopefully, to comfort her. Upon their arrival on the appropriate floor, the group was met at the elevator by the smiling mother. With profound gratitude she proceeded to thank them for coming such a long distance on such short notice to pray for her and her little girl, and for helping her daughter to die in peace. She then shared her recent decision that she was going to dedicate the rest of her life to helping other parents and children going through similar situations to cope with their ordeal.

Clearly her daughter had fulfilled her sun-path, a powerful example of greater good arising from the ashes of a personal tragedy to benefit future generations.

In addition to the gift of a unique talent, the second of the two gifts to help us serve the Creator more effectively concerns our ability to communicate with fellow human beings, with animals, and perhaps even with plants in a very special way that is not connected to our physical being. This involves the Ojibway concept of the soul-spirit. It is a combination of our own soul and the Aura or Spirit of the Creator.

It is what makes us alive and eternal, and is responsible for our own personal and unique soul.

Through this soul-spirit, human beings have the ability to communicate in a special way, for we are all related to and part of one another. Traditional Indian people converse in this way—not physical body to physical body, which is the shallow, impersonal talk heard most often at cocktail-parties—but soul-spirit to soul-spirit. This is done in a non-physical manner, sometimes with words being exchanged aloud and sometimes without. This can take place not only between humans but also, it is believed by traditional northeastern American Indian people, between humans and animals, humans and plants, and plants and animals. An example, as I have mentioned earlier, is the spoken prayers of apology for harvesting plants and killing animals, in which Indian people talk directly to the soul-spirit of the plant or animal.

In addition to the spoken word, it is now an accepted scientific fact that two types of silent communication can and do exist: extrasensory perception, called ESP, and precognition. Scientists continue to study this phenomenon, for how this happens is still a mystery, as far as I know.

Soul-spirit to soul-spirit communication—or ESP—involves events occurring at the time. It is often referred to as mental telepathy. ESP is a relatively common phenomenon. For example, many of us have experienced the following events: two people, together or even apart, have the same thought using the same words at the same time; or a person reaches for the telephone to call a friend they have not seen or talked to for years, only to have the phone ring and find it is that person calling.

Precognition, or extrasensory perception of events that will occur in the future, is a less common form of soul-spirit to soul-spirit communication. Again, to Indians precognition is not an uncommon phenomenon and may concern either the person's life or someone else's. For instance, according to tradition, usually by way of a vision from the Creator, a person may be blessed with the knowledge of when they will pass over in the future and given guidance as to what they are meant to do in the meantime. This is usually some unfinished or even some new service for the Creator and is called a death quest. A person may also be blessed with the foreknowledge of events or occurrences that will happen to other people.

In addition to ESP and precognition, there is a third type of silent soul-spirit to soul-spirit communication that occurs between a deceased and a living person and has long been experienced by northeastern Native American people. As yet to my knowledge, this phenomenon has not been proved to the satisfaction of the general scientific community.

I have witnessed some very interesting and powerful experiences of soul-spirit communications. While we all have had ESP experiences, I'd like to share with you one that stand out in my mind to show how powerful they can be.

This involves a typical ESP experience my wife and I had on an ongoing basis with Del Logan. Del was a diabetic, had heart trouble, and lived alone on the Onondaga reservation in Nedrow, New York. Occasionally, despite her best efforts, she was too far from her one telephone when she would begin to go into a diabetic attack, and she would then get in touch with my wife and me telepathically, or soul-spirit to soul-spirit, over a distance of more than 200 miles. Both Debbie and I would suddenly become very nervous and find ourselves calling the hospital to see if we could help her. Del's return call from the emergency room of a Syracuse hospital on one occasion says it all: "Got your attention that time, didn't I!"

Subsequently, on August 1, 1978, a young woman who was related to Del called my wife and me to tell us that Del had died from a diabetic attack terminating in cardiac arrest. We were devastated. How had we not heard her? When we arrived at the funeral, the same young woman quickly sought us out to convey a message that Del asked her to deliver to us shortly before she passed over. Del wanted us to know that she had done everything she could for us and everything she was meant to do in this life, and that it was time for her to join the circle of her ancestors. We should not blame ourselves for not hearing her; she had deliberately refrained from contacting us!

Several examples of the soul-spirit to soul-spirit communication, called precognition today, involved Del as well. The first was in the form of a death quest granted by the Creator. Although her premonition of passing over did not manifest itself in the dramatic way of a vision, it nonetheless filled her with a sudden sense of purpose and urgency. I shall never forget the day she came to me in haste— extremely unusual for her—and made an offer that was both unexpected and unsolicited. Always going right to the heart of what was on her mind, she said, "I have been asked to write a book about the Old Way of my people by the Museum of the American Indian, the Smithsonian, and other museums, but the time was never right. Now I feel I must do this for your museum, if you are willing to see that it is published—and in the appropriate way, through our people's crafts. Only in this way may I share our beliefs."

Willing? I was ecstatic, but how could we do it and where would the money come from? Almost a year went by, and then Del's manuscript unexpectedly arrived in the mail. It was hastily but beautifully written. Her prose was essentially a reflection of how she spoke, not in a form most of us would employ to write. It was lyrical and with little punctuation—almost a stream of consciousness in the beginning—but *so* powerful. I could just hear Del saying the words to me, as she did so often during our times together. And she had illustrated her book for us in her own way, as well. Shortly thereafter a grant from *Reader's Digest* arrived with the stipulation that it be used to pay for our publication of three books of our choice, provided the proceeds be put into an endowment fund to pay for future publications. We had the precious book and we had the money! But before we could even get a copy back to Del with our editing suggestions, she had passed over to join her ancestors. After much soul-searching we decided to publish this book as she had written it, with our editors making changes only where punctuation was essential to convey the power of Del's words. *Memories of Sweet Grass* is a chronicle of her life.

The other type of precognitive power, a foretelling of another person's future is illustrated by a gift Del gave to me that she called a "life-string." It was composed of hand-made shell beads, drilled and threaded onto a native, hemp-like material. The top one, Del told me, fingering the beads to remember the story each told, was a purple bead, the bead of my birth. A fiber knot separated the birth-bead from the next series of beads of about one inch, representing my childhood years then another knot before the next series of four white beads of slightly different sizes, which Del said indicated the achievements of my teens and twenties: dedicating my life to Mother Earth in college and graduate school, my work to educate people of many ages to be stewards of Creation, and my interest in all things related to the Creator. Another knot was followed by eleven more white beads, each of which Del said was in recognition of accomplishments in my thirties and forties. According to Del, these included my vision to start the Indian Institute, my dedication to helping Indian people and Gunnery students, taking children into our family and home, and my services as a volunteer in area towns. Another knot in the string was followed by sixteen beads. Since Del gave me this gift in 1977, the predictions involving this and the last bead section were made using her precognitive powers, although all she said to me, in her understated way, was that this section was my future lifeline. She said the sixteen-bead section was to represent my fifties and sixties, the busiest and most productive time of my life, and, of course, this turned out to be true. This time was the zenith of my services to the Indian Institute and to the surrounding communities. I also completed other important tasks, including taking the Institute's message to local, state, and national groups, conventions, and scientific symposia; and writing articles for state and national publications. This culminated in my being included in *Who's Who in the World,* a Western status symbol to be sure, but an honor in those days, and one which benefited the Institute's and my credibility with non-Indian people whom we wanted to reach with our mission of faith and cultural understanding.

One final knot near the bottom of the string was followed by a fawn toe bone, representing, according to Del, a major achievement in my seventies or eighties. I asked her what this could be. It was something personal, she told me. She could not see it clearly, but this event would happen, would be of great import, and would be related to the Indian Institute. I asked her if the completion of this task also signaled my demise, as it was the end of the string; and Del said that at the moment she could see no further than this significant event and that she might be blessed with further insight in the future.

Ned Swigart's Life String and Water Drum,
Gifts of Del Logan

These were our last words on the subject of my life-string. I have waited many years for the reality of her prediction to manifest itself, for I was certain it would. Now this story takes on a life of its own, complete with its inherent miracles and human angels. It has become a culmination of everything I believe and everything I wish to share, and I am convinced that the publication of this book about my northeastern American Indian faith, clearly linked to the Institute as it is, is what Del foresaw so many years ago!

In addition to ESP and precognition, there is a third type of soul-spirit to soul-spirit communication, this one between a living person and a person who has already passed over. One of the most dramatic incidents that I have ever experienced involved an event that occurred at the Indian Institute while I was director there. One evening two of my Native American teachers and I were working late at the Institute. At approximately six o'clock a car pulled into the driveway. Out stepped several people, including a very elderly, very slender, very short Aztec man, and another man who explained that he would act as interpreter, since this Aztec elder, whose name in English was the Maestro, spoke neither Spanish nor English. The Aztec elder stopped halfway up the front walk to the museum and went into a trance-like state. A few moments later he resumed walking and said through the translator, "This is a sacred place." I agreed, passing on the information that elders from all over the northern hemisphere who came to visit our center offered prayers to the Creator blessing the museum and its work. We entered the museum, and the Maestro began to hurry about, pointing out specific items in the main exhibit hall that he said had been blessed: an Iroquois ceremonial mask, several pipes, and a war club—all of which had belonged to Native Americans of various northeastern Indian nations revered by their people. The Maestro was unfamiliar with the specific people who had owned the items, but he knew that they were blessed. He clearly felt the Aura from them.

Then the Maestro did an astounding thing. He moved quickly, and largely unguided, through a series of doors, through our shop, and into our storage room containing more than a million artifacts. We stopped at one of the cabinets that contained our ethnographic materials. I opened it for him, and in the bottom drawer was a jacket labeled "Sioux." He again went into a prayer-trance and, after several moments of complete quiet, leapt forward and placed an offering of tobacco in the drawer, saying through the interpreter, "This is Sitting Bull's Jacket. Who is Sitting Bull?"

The two staff members and I were amazed but did not doubt this revelation, although we knew that many university-trained professional curators would not accept it as fact. I explained to the Maestro that Sitting Bull was a famous medicine man and leader of the Hunkpapa Teton Sioux, greatly respected and loved by his people. In 1890 on the Standing Rock Reservation in South Dakota, Sitting Bull and his son were shot and killed in his wigwam by police enlisted by the US government from among his own people because leaders in Washington, DC, were concerned he wanted to renew the Indian Wars, which he had no intention of doing.

After our visitors left the museum that night, I determined to attempt to trace the ownership of this jacket that the Maestro had identified as belonging to Sitting Bull. Here was a supreme example of soul-spirit to soul-spirit communication between a living Indian and one who had already passed over. If I could find additional proof that curators might be more likely to accept, I thought I could establish the potential authenticity of this mode of identification. I remembered from my days as chairman of the board of the Gunn Memorial Museum, where we stored our Indian collections before the Institute was built, that the jacket donor was Ruth Hull Cornell. She had grown up in Minneapolis, Minnesota, and now lived in our town of Washington. She was the mother of a friend of mine. When I called Ruth, her opening remark to me was "You are calling about Sitting Bull's jacket." I asked how she knew it was Sitting Bull's, as it was not listed as such in our Indian Institute records or on the jacket itself. She related the following story her father had told her and which she, in turn, had passed on to her son.

Ruth Hull Cornell's father, Louis K. Hull, went to Yale University as a freshman in 1879 and graduated in 1883. There he met and became a close friend (and roommate, Ruth believed) of Frederic Remington who had entered Yale's School of Fine Arts in 1878. Remington left college at age nineteen, halfway through his sophomore year, and soon moved west to try his hand at any number of different jobs, but he always kept in close touch with Ruth's father. When Louis Hull finished college, he followed Remington westward, settling in Minneapolis, Minnesota, where Remington was a regular visitor in the

Hull home. The two men remained close personal friends for the rest of their lives. Remington loved the West and recorded what he saw there in drawings, paintings, and sculpture of soldiers, cowboys, Indians—everything to do with Western life. In the process Remington became, according to Ruth Hull Cornell, a friend of Sitting Bull.

The next part of Ruth Cornell's story established the connection between Sitting Bull, Frederic Remington, Louis Hull, Ruth Hull Cornell, the Gunn Memorial Library and Museum, and the jacket's current home at the Institute.

Ruth Hull Cornell told me that according to her father, Sitting Bull's wife had given his jacket, in love, to Remington after her husband's assassination. Some eighteen years later, shortly before Mr. Remington's death from appendicitis in 1909 at the age of forty-eight, he, in turn, had passed this jacket on, in love, to Ruth's father, his very special friend. Her father had passed it on to her, in love, and eventually, she passed it on to the Gunn Memorial Library and Museum in Washington, Connecticut. The Gunn Museum in turn had passed this jacket on to Indian Institute on permanent loan for safekeeping in our alarm-protected and special humidity and temperature-controlled facility. Somewhere during these transfers the jacket had had its identification label changed to remove the name of Sitting Bull, purportedly because of a lack of supportive information.

With this new evidence in hand, I contacted a friend and former staff member of Indian Institute, Ann McMullen, PhD, who is the current curator of Indian collections for the Smithsonian Institute's Museum of the American Indian. I asked Ann's opinion about the additional, potentially corroborating evidence that Ruth Hull Cornell provided concerning the Sitting Bull jacket story. Given Ann's inherently conservative curatorial attitude, was Ruth's story as significant to her as it was to a number of us at Institute and in the Indian community?

I received the following answer from Ann the next day. Our e-mail exchange in August of 2004 speaks clearly of the dilemma of establishing ground rules for acceptable evidence in the museum world today, and how one deals with the different perspectives on this issue ranging from traditional Native Americans, on the one hand, to museum people trained from a Western world-perspective, on the other:

> Ned:
> Since I can safely say that every museum I've worked in since 1978—no matter how large or small—has had purported Sitting Bull objects in its collections, I take all such attributions with a hefty grain of salt. The Cornell story is interesting, but Remington did not move permanently to the West in the 1880s but instead vacillated between Canton, N.Y. [where he was born] and Kansas City, with some trips to the West. His documented long trips were to Arizona and New Mexico, not the Dakotas, although he certainly may have made it to Montana briefly. No part of his biography that I've seen suggests that he spent appreciable time at Standing Rock or that he knew Sitting Bull. As an enterprising fellow, Remington would surely have written about Sitting Bull in one of his books or articles (less well known than his paintings and bronzes) even if he didn't paint or draw him at this early period of his career. Sitting Bull, especially under the circumstances, would have been fodder for Remington's writings.
>
> Without corroborating evidence from Remington's or Sitting Bull's life events (which don't seem to jibe), this Cornell story could not be considered reasonable evidence that the jacket belonged to Sitting Bull. The connection between the Hulls and Remington seems clear, but the Remington and Sitting Bull part needs work.
>
> If it sounds like I am too well versed in this kind of stuff, it is because I spent some time over the past few months investigating whether a drum and several other items in NMAI's [National Museum of the American Indian's] collection belonged to Sitting Bull.
> My opinion,
> Ann[6]

Despite Ann's views I felt compelled to continue my research and was fortunate to find more potential pieces of evidence soon thereafter. The first concerned information that Remington apparently did travel through the Dakotas according to a 1977 publication about *the Buffalo Bill Historical Center* in Cody, Wyoming, stating Remington had tried a number of different jobs "...first as a sheep rancher, saloon-keeper and itinerant cowpuncher in Montana, Kansas and the Dakotas before establishing himself as a prolific illustrator and artist."[7]

The second potential piece of evidence was a positive identification by Arval Rogers, Cheyenne scholar and artist, who, after careful examination of our jacket, in October of 2004 sent me a copy of a picture labeled "1885 albumen print by David F. Barry of Sitting Bull." In the picture Sitting Bull was wearing a jacket that Arval describes in an inscription on a copy of the photo as "exactly like it" (the jacket at the Institute).

To see if this additional information was helpful, I again asked Ann for her comments. She sent the following e-mail response:

> Ned:
> These fragments still don't add up to a convincing case for the jacket.
>
> According to some sources Remington was traveling in the West in 1887, and Sitting Bull may have been at Standing Rock, or was traveling with the Buffalo Bill show that year (he supposedly turned down the 1887 trip to Europe, but an English newspaper from December 1887 says he was there, or this might have been his son, also called Sitting Bull). He did go to DC in 1888 about reservation lands. Remington's writings still do not record that they met, and for me that information is most persuasive.
>
> As for D.F. Barry, there are at least four D.F. Barry photos of Sitting Bull, and the one where he is wearing that kind of jacket is tentatively dated 1884, 1885, or 1888. Also not convincing unless there is an absolute side-by-side comparison. While at IAIS, I did compare the jacket to that photo, and I was not convinced.
> Best,
> Ann[8]

While I find that from my own perspective I am more inclined to accept the position that evidence does exist to suggest that this was indeed Sitting Bull's jacket, I can respect, as a genealogist and scientist, the latter one that Ann represents. I still pray for many reasons, including its importance to the faith of Native American people, that the final documentation Ann needs is out there somewhere waiting to be found.

As for this spiritually gifted Aztec gentleman, I later was told that as he was returning to Mexico, he was drawn to take a side trip to Kansas City where he was given the power to recognize a previously unidentified pipe in a museum there as belonging to Sitting Bull. These identifications of Sitting Bull's personal items would be termed impossibly miraculous in our Western world, but communication between the spirits of people here on Earth and the spirits of people who have passed over are part of the northeastern Native American faith.

In addition to soul-spirit communication between living human beings and, many traditional Indians believe, between human beings and those of people who have passed over, there is the belief among northeastern Native people that humans can communicate with animal and plant soul-spirits as well.

We of Indian faith hope these will also be proved to the satisfaction of the scientific community. There does seem to be some evidence that might lead to such proof starting with the commonality of all living tissue. In a practical and a scientific sense, living things share the same cellular parts and cellular activities, including the still-mysterious gift of life. Thus is it not possible that if we can communicate with fellow human beings this way, might we also be able to do so with other living things, both animal and plant? I, and many people who have had interactions with household pets and wild animals, believe the former may very well occur, as my experiences, for instance, with wolves and deer suggest, and that this connection may well be proved scientifically in time.

While human-plant communication has been proved to be a more difficult matter to research, there continue to be people in the Western world attempting to look into the possibility with, arguably, some success. Some have attempted new technologies and different (and, to many scientists, often unorthodox) methods to get to the core of this supposition. For instance, Dr. Cleve Backster,[9] whom I first read about in the 1960s, tried to apply his expertise with lie detector equipment registering human emotions to the problem of whether plants would also show emotional activity when tested with this same equipment in the same way and under the same stress-related factors. His published results were met with some acceptance and excitement, but overwhelming criticism by the majority of the scientific community that argued that by not using the scientific method of testing a hypothesis, the study rendered the results invalid. Fortunately efforts continue to prove a human-plant connection, which I hope happens for the sake of scientifically verifying what traditional northeastern American Indians already believe. The Native American traditional belief that individual uniqueness occurs has been proved scientifically. Native American and Western ESP and precognition powers are being researched and are considered by many as very possible if not true. Communication with animals is being increasingly accepted. Is it not reasonable, then, that human and animal communication with plants is also possible? My Indian faith says yes.

Chapter 9

The Longhouse Classroom

Let us now pass through the door into the replicated longhouse classroom. This facility was blessed and dedicated to Del Logan shortly after her passing over in 1978. Onondaga friends made the long journey to honor her in this special way, and Mohawk people conducted the traditional dedication service. Numerous other Native Americans from different nations, both in the northeast and from other parts of the country, and staff and board members of the Indian Institute also attended.

Longhouse Classroom and Mural of Village Activity

The original longhouse, since enlarged to fill the entire room, was built of local materials by Del with the help of area school children and was largely furnished by Del and her Onondaga friends. You will notice that footprints of common animals and birds used in various ways by Indian people are impressed in the earth-colored, concrete floor, and painted on the wall to your right is a full-length mural depicting the life of the northeastern Native people who would have lived in this longhouse and the nearby wigwams.

This is Del's home now; here, as elder-teachers, she and her guest and friend Keewaydinoquay will eternally pass on the culture and faith of their Iroquoian and Ojibway people.

In this longhouse classroom you will see how northeastern American Indians actually lived before 1492, how their activities were based on the people's role as stewards of Mother Earth, and how constant reminders of the Creator were found in every aspect of their lives.

Notice immediately the many furnishings stored on and under the bed-shelves fastened to the longhouse walls and scattered about the dwelling. Here we see berry baskets, white birch and splint containers, a water drum, three-dimensional twig decoys used in hunting geese and ducks, a beautiful beaver-skin vest, a woman's skirt and blouse, numerous bowls, bark containers, and assorted tools, as well as a number of treated animal pelts from such mammals as beaver, deer, bear, wolf, and fox. Various dried herbs, medicinal plants, berries, and such food crops as corn are suspended from the ceiling to be used when necessary.

Over there on the right in the middle of the cornfield, a very young boy occupies a platform from sunrise to sunset to scare away crows and whatever creatures might come to steal corn, and to be alert for any danger that might threaten the village. Older men, unable to do a day's manual work, are assigned to tasks like this as well. Remember, boys, from the age of five, are traditionally considered old enough to begin to assume a man's duties, and everyone in this village works for the Creator and the common good of all.

Replicated Northeastern American Indian Village before White Contact
(at Institute for American Indian Studies)

You can tell what time of the year a wigwam has been constructed by materials that are used to cover it. See, over there is a dwelling covered with elm bark. The Ojibway and the Iroquois often used elm bark. A dwelling of this kind is made in the spring when the bark is loosest and easiest to peel off a tree. Near that wigwam is a dwelling covered with rushes that are available at other seasons, when bark is not. As you can see, these dwellings are snug, and water and wind-proof. A layer of skins would line the interior to provide insulation in winter, and a small, central hearth-fire was kept burning to make the occupants quite warm and comfortable, even in the worst of weather. Note, this house is fully biodegradable, a popular term and a popular cause these days, but an element of northeastern American Indian life for many generations.

Now notice the girdled trees over there, the ones with the bark removed from the base of the tree. See how practical this is? Girdling effectively kills the tree and leaves it standing to age for future use as firewood. Its roots can continue to hold the soil, instead of the tree lying on the ground to rot or being immediately burned to clear a field as European settlers have done for generations.

Replicated Northeastern American Indian Garden before White Contact
(at Institute for American Indian Studies)

And over there you can see how the crops, the "Three Sisters"—corn, beans, and squash—are planted in the traditional "hill method" that northeastern American Indian people used and we have duplicated here at the Institute in our Indian Garden. The Iroquois, and all northeastern peoples living in a climate suitable to grow these crops, followed the same procedure. First, people cleared the land, leaving the previously girdled dead trees. Then, with hoes made of wood or made using a wooden handle with a hoe-shaped stone fastened to its end, they made a series of small hills. From seeds carefully selected from the very best plants grown the previous year, Indian people usually grouped several varieties of domesticated plants together, the corn kernels in the center of the hill, and the bean seeds surrounding it. The bean roots added nitrogen to the soil, fertilizing the corn, and the bean plants climbed up the corn. Squash were planted on the outside of the circle. These were also fertilized by the beans, and the squash's large leaves had an added benefit of covering the ground between the hills, helping to prevent erosion and the growth of native plant species (such as raspberry and blackberry), as these would compete unfavorably with the domesticated plants.

The furnishings in the longhouse and the activities you see on the mural on the wall tell us so much about the northeastern American Indian sense of stewardship. Let us take food, for example. As you now know, Del's people and other northeastern Native Americans only killed what meat they could eat or preserve. A large deer, elk, moose, or even buffalo, was shared by the family who had made the kill with those in need; shared at a big party for all the neighbors; or dried and smoked on racks built over a fire for storage as "jerky." Jerky was a valuable resource used as a food supplement during travel or saved for wintertime. Fish were readily available in the spring, summer, and fall. To catch them, northeastern American Indian people used weirs to channel the fish, as well as nets, spears, fish traps, and even wooden plugs as lures, and twig and bone fishhooks. After catching the fish, those that were not immediately eaten were dried and smoked and stored for the winter, when food was scarce. Some of the best places to fish were at natural falls where spawning fish would congregate in the spring and fall. For instance, the Weantinoge in what is now New Milford, Connecticut, and the Schaghticoke at Kent had a wonderful spot to fish at the Great Falls in New Milford. There they gathered from the surrounding countryside to spear shad during the spring spawning run from Long Island Sound.

In winter Indians had Mother Earth's natural freezer. This time of year, therefore, was when they killed most of the larger animals like deer, moose, and elk. Then, if they had extra meat, they simply hung it as high as possible in a tree to prevent dogs and other creatures from reaching it, and the meat would quickly freeze.

As for storing plant foods, look around you in this longhouse. Food is stored in large amounts to last through as much of the winter as possible. Indian people would go to hickory and white oak stands in the fall to pick up nuts which were stored in longhouses, storage houses, and even underground storage pits lined with cedar bark to repel pests and insects. Fruit like strawberries, raspberries, and blueberries would be picked in the spring and summer, dried on mats on the ground, and stored for winter use. Major agricultural food crops such as corn, beans, and squash were also stored for winter, the corn hung in the rafters of longhouses, placed in specially made corncribs, or even put underground in cedar- and other evergreen-lined pits.

Concerning non-agricultural plants, the wild potato was harvested in the fall and then stored as the agricultural crops were. A number of other native plant roots, tubers, stems, fruits, and herbs were harvested during the fall and stored. These included the wild sumac berries that I have already mentioned and yellow water lily roots. Only a few plants were readily available in winter, but they were very important. Among them were the previously mentioned white pine, whose cambium was nutritious to eat, and the white pine and hemlock needles, which provided a nutritious tea rich in vitamin C. There were also a number of different plant species whose bark could be used, such as the spicebush for flavoring food, and yellow and black birch bark for teas tasting like root beer.

Northeastern American Indians also had to have a good supply of medicinal herbs for the winter. Leaves, stems, and roots of various plants were collected in the summer, and dried and hung in the rafters for winter use.

Potable water was in constant demand, and Native people chose year-round and winter living sites beside streams that flowed rapidly enough not to freeze. Their favorite place was where such a stream entered a river or lake because these rivers and lakes not only furnished large amounts of food in season, but they also became the Indian's main "roads" between their villages—by canoe in summer and by snowshoe in winter.

Interestingly, northeastern American Indians were purported to have had none of the communicable diseases known in Europe until the coming of the white man. Introduced white diseases, like smallpox, brought by early European explorers and fisherman even before the white colonists came to settle in the northeast, ravaged Indian populations that had no immunity to these diseases. Personal hygiene and un-crowded, relatively sanitary living conditions are a few of the reasons thought to be responsible for the Indian's lack of communicable diseases until that time. For instance Native Americans had a practice of taking some sort of a "bath" almost every day, such as sweat baths or rolling in the snow in winter, and plunging into the water, no matter how cold, the year round. The early European settlers, however, had an aversion for water, believing at the time that it caused or resulted in illness, rather than the other way around. Also the Indians used the natural, undisturbed landscape as a way of recycling all human waste that came from foods they had "borrowed" initially from Mother Earth, rather than throwing waste out the windows onto the stone-paved city streets as many Europeans did.

Regarding tools and clothing, northeastern American Indian people made their own when they were needed. Wood, stone, and other essential natural materials were everywhere, gifts of the Creator and Mother Earth. As I mentioned earlier, non-Indian people don't know what wonderful clothes Native people had until they've worn moccasins, pants, shirts, and skirts made of indescribably soft, smooth doeskin or heavier buckskin made by traditional brain-tanning and hide-working methods. Notice the buck and doeskin garments around the longhouse.

Each family had their indoor fire in the middle of the floor so that all the heat could be disseminated throughout the family's living space, and they clustered around the fire in a circle. Remember, all northeastern American Indian life is conducted in this circle, in harmony with others and with their world. Think of the white way of heating a house with wood during these early times and even during the modern era. A huge stone, brick, or (during colonial times) a fireplace made of twigs and mud was usually built at one end of a cabin or house. The fireplace had to be piled high with wood because the fire would lose almost all of its heat up the chimney before it could adequately warm even a small part of the house.

Notice that through all of the activities of daily living present in this mural and in this longhouse, the central theme is always carrying on what the elders had taught younger generations about remaining as one with the world, keeping needs in balance with surroundings, and returning themselves and all the products of their lives to Mother Earth from whence they came.

Now that we have completed our overview of the northeastern American Indian culture as it is graphically presented in this, Del's room, it is most appropriate to give Keewaydinoquay and Adelphena "Del" Logan's personal stories about their lives, so closely aligned with the lessons of our longhouse classroom.

Chapter 10

Keewaydinoquay's and Adelphena Logan's Personal Stories

Come sit here on this bench with me for a moment. With Del's permission and the permission of members of Keewaydinoquay's family, I am deeply honored to share with you the stories of their lives as told to me by the two of them over the years.

As I have mentioned, many northeastern Native Americans see birth and passing over as the two defining moments of their existence, the beginning and the end of life as they know it on Mother Earth. They spend the time between these two events in a journey of self-discovery, seeking to learn why they are here and what they are meant to do by virtue of their unique inheritance to serve the Creator, their brothers and sisters, and all of the Creator's world.

First, let me share Kee's personal sun-path journey, which is similar in many respects to other northeastern American Indians with one notable exception: During a time when many Indian people neither desired nor were able to pursue a white man's education, Kee managed to do this. Otherwise, her life was filled with the normal ups and downs of living, but with added complicating factors of being Native American by birth and attempting to live a traditional Ojibway life surrounded by people following Western white cultural practices and beliefs.

Kee was born in 1918 on a freighter on Lake Michigan. At birth, Kee became a member of the Crane Clan of the Miniss Kitigan (Gardner Island) Band of the Ojibway Anishinaabeg. Her parents were of Anishinaabeg-Scottish-English roots. She spent most of her childhood living on Cathead Bay in Northern Michigan, near the Beaver Archipelago.

Keewaydinoquay, Ojibway
(Painting by David Wagner)

According to Kee, an Ojibway baby is traditionally given a baby name, for her people feel it is silly to call someone by an adult name when they are a small child and have not yet earned an appropriate name from adult life skills and accomplishments. How Kee received such a baby name is a wonderful story. Her mother had a white name, which pleased her grandfather, an Anglican missionary, very much. But her father had an Indian name and wanted one for Kee. It was customary for an Ojibway child to have an infant name by the age of nine months, so the child could have their own identity before the parents had another child. However, Kee still had no baby name when she was about eighteen months old until one day when the women of her family went to pick blueberries. Kee was taken along by her mother who put her on a blanket on the ground and went off to join the other women as they began to harvest berries. When they returned, the baby was not on the blanket. Then they saw her standing between two bears, raking blueberries off the bushes just like the bears. The women did not dare to interrupt this scene, hoping that when the bears wandered off, they would leave the baby. The bears eventually moved to another bush, but she went with them. Finally the bears moved away, and Kee was reunited with her family.

From that time on, until she was a woman and given a woman's name, her baby name became "Walks With Bears." Some baby names, such as this, are complimentary; others are not, but everyone knows the child name is only temporary.

At an early age, Kee became dedicated to the ceremonial drum of her band, a gift from her grandfather to care for after he died; it was a very sacred responsibility for her for the rest of her life.

> Much of my early childhood was spent along Cathead Bay, which is now a part of Leelanau County, Michigan. On one occasion an Anishinaabeg traveling to the lumber camps stopped at our place to tell my father to come immediately for a funeral feast on Garden Island....One of my mother's objections to the journey had been her desire to keep me from contact with the "pagan" religion, for she was the daughter of an Anglican missionary. Accordingly, I was left in the care of...Joe Peet...who had been told that he could not attend the feast [either], and neither of us liked the situation, but disobedience was not part of our upbringing. However, Joe Peet threatened to lock me into a small cellar under a trap door in the middle of the cabin floor if I didn't behave. Frightened, I ran off down the woodland cart trail in the direction my parents had taken....Long before I reached my destination, I could hear the sound of a great drum and the rise and fall of many voices. It echoed from the bay behind Little Island, and sounded like two drums and thousands of people, a sound unknown that reached out to create a spirit throbbing in my blood. Rounding Catfish Cove I saw a cortege of men bared to the waist carrying the deceased's [body] to the northwest and a multitude of people retiring the Drum to the East.
>
> 'Baum! Home!' the muffled slow-measured Drum said. 'Little-Walks-With-Bears-Woman, welcome to your heart's home!' This was my first sight of a large group of people moving rhythmically to a drum. I had never danced. My maternal grandfather felt dancing was sinful. But without hesitation I began dancing

with a group of girls my age who were in the procession retiring the Drum to the East. It was there that a greatly disturbed mother found me, scolded me thoroughly and laid on me a punishment of learning a chapter of scripture. It was duly learned—to the rhythm of the Drum, which still beats inside my brain. Nothing else mattered. It had Happened; The Drum has guided my life ever since.[10]

When Kee was nine years old, she was accepted for training as a member of the secret and powerful healing society of her people known as the Midewewin, or Grand Medicine Society, and she told me she had never felt prouder than on that occasion. As an initiation rite and to experience a vision, she had to paddle a canoe as far as she could—to the point of risking death from exertion (this type of physical self-abuse was banned by the Ojibway in 1978). Some initiates paddled 500 miles before they might have an experience of deep meaning—a vision. Kee finally had one, and hers was of being drowned and returning to life.

After Kee's return, as per Ojibway custom, she was apprenticed with an Anishinaabeg herbalist and healer, Nodjimahkwe. Nodjimahkwe was a highly respected female member of the Midewewin, and prepared her apprentice well for her work with this society. Kee related to me that she was very fortunate to walk her own path at that young an age, for often a child was apprenticed to a person who was known for what the parents wanted their child to do, not for what the child may have wished.

According to Ojibway tradition, when girls and boys reached puberty, they took very separate paths. From the time they were small, Kee and the other girls her age were taught that the Creator had granted them the supreme human gift of being able to bear children, a privilege carried out for the Ojibway people, and that pain was a natural part of this privilege. Therefore, when a young girl was experiencing her first menstruation, she went off into the woods alone with great delight and joy, not because any of her people thought it was "dirty" or did not want to be with her. On this occasion, Kee went into the woods to be free to think, to meditate, to pray, to thank the Creator, and to accept this great gift—she was fertile now and was able to bear children! When Kee returned, there was a great celebration, and she then became a full-fledged member of her community with all the rights of membership, including the pursuit of a vision if she so desired. The baby name no longer applied to her, and an adult name was given in honor of this event. The name given to her was Keewaydinoquay, or "Woman of the North Wind." To her people this symbolized her future sun-path, coming from a direction of great mystery, a place of dreaming and becoming anew.

Thereafter, when Kee had her monthly period, she joined the other women who went to a special sweat lodge that had been built for them. It was located in a secluded, serene spot, had a particular shape and position, and used heated rocks to keep the interior warm but not as hot as a regular sweat lodge. Kee looked forward to her "week off" every four weeks, and to getting an aunt or a grandmother to care for the family while she was gone. During this week, not only was Kee freed from the heavy burdens of her life and in a serene place with no worries, but also she had better food and accommodations than usual, and made life-long, close friendships in this relaxed atmosphere with other women who were there every month with her.

Unlike girls, boys who reached the age of puberty had to actively engage in a number of physical endurance tests and undertake a vision quest as a vision was essential for a man to follow his sun-path. We'll talk about this later.

As for Kee's personal life during her later years, she told me she would like to have said that she walked the sun-trail and had been an herbalist all of her life, but it was difficult to have a smooth journey, free of doubts and wanderings up other paths that turned out to be false leads or dead ends. Her journey was made doubly difficult by the increasing white presence and influence on the traditional Indian way of life in the area where she lived. This was especially true early on in her adult years, when white people persuaded Kee that the terrible things that had been happening to her—her husband abandoning her, the state taking her child, and many other events—were the result of her being an Indian and practicing the Old Way of the traditional Ojibway people. So Kee tried to become white. She married a white man and had four children. Two followed the Indian spirit way, and the other two were Christians. But as Kee tried to walk the way of the white man, she saw beloved people get ill and she felt only the Indian medicine of her people could heal them. Finally she returned to the Indian way to pursue once again her calling as an herbalist.

While Kee was going through this life-way change, she went to a white college to learn to be a teacher. Later she went on to study plant medicines, at the University of Michigan. And she also had the most wonderful experience of working with the great ethno-botanist Dr. Richard S. Shultes at the Harvard Botanical Museum. He was the person, she told me, who urged her to write a book that he helped to get published. It was titled *Puhpohwee for the People: A Narrative Account of Some Uses of Fungi among the Anishinaabeg* and was published in 1978 by the Harvard University Press.

Then late in her life when she was visiting the Indian Institute for a special occasion, she shared with me her sudden realization that she must pass on, apparently as a death quest, this vast compendium of wild plant-healing knowledge in her remaining days or much of it would be lost. I jotted down her words, as I frequently did with all of my elder-teachers.

> I now realize that my knowledge of plants for medicinal use is a fast disappearing part of our Ojibway life. We have become westernized to the extent of using white drugs to cure essentially white diseases that our people are increasingly prone to catch because we had little or no natural immunity to these illnesses. Why, even such relatively minor white childhood illnesses as chickenpox and measles have often proved fatal to our people. But in doing this, we are quickly forgetting about our long history of wonderful medicines to treat the body ailments that we traditionally suffered. In this regard, I believed I

am called now as a service to the Creator to attempt to pass these traditional healing medicines on to other people, not necessarily Indian people, but anyone who has the deep commitment to preserve and use this heritage.

I set about trying to find just the right person or people to come and stay with me on the island and let me teach them of these things. Many have come. I asked you, too, Ned, do you remember? But you had received your vision, and you had to remain true to that. However, as much as I hoped and prayed that the right person would come, and I asked many young people whom I thought would be perfect, at the last moment I could not bring myself to share my information. They would stay awhile and then leave, saddened, as I was. I actually did share a lot of information with many people, but, much to my disappointment, I have never found that one special person. This is just not "meant to be," after all. But when I see all that you, Ned, and others have done here at the Indian Institute and elsewhere, how you have put what I shared with you and taught you to such wonderful use, I see that I have indeed served as the Creator's steward in a way I did not fully recognize until recently.

In addition to bringing this revered place into existence, Ned, I must thank you for carrying on my great interest in Native plants. My sharing what I did with you about plant medicines really made you take action, didn't it?[11]

Indeed it had.

After first hearing from Kee of the great plant medicines Indian people had to treat diseases we of the Western world did not have cures for, and then recognizing the fear Kee had that these would be lost to the human race, I took it upon myself to call on several pharmaceutical companies. I had become acquainted with their top people in my quest for Indian Institute funding, and wanted to share this knowledge with them. My plan was to enlist their help in verifying the worth and then making available some of the northeastern American Indian's most important medications, which were not available to the general public at the time.

Essentially their answers were all the same. They were in the business of saving lives and were pursuing new medicines all the time, including Native American ones. However, research was so expensive and federal controls were so stringent that if they were to prepare a drug from the United States and Canada and it was a native plant easily found and utilized, there was a danger that people would end up learning how to use the native plant and therefore not buy their synthetic drug. So they have studied and developed medicines from South America, Native American drugs like the very effective myacin family of "wonder drugs" that are complex and relatively difficult to access, and it is these they now sell all over the world. And, finally, they were indeed in the business of saving lives, but were also in the business, like it or not, of making money for their investors.

Kee followed her sun-path, as difficult as this was for her at times. She bore children. She enriched the lives of other children with her training as a teacher. Her service, not only as an herbalist but also as a renowned healer and teacher, was a gift to all mankind, as was her commitment to sharing, wherever possible, as much information as she could, both orally and in written form, about plants and plant medicines for future generations. Once she returned to her sun-path, she dedicated herself fully to it until she passed over in 1999.

I will now share with you the story of Adelphena Logan's life in the Onondaga Iroquois tradition. Del, unlike Kee, was very reticent about sharing such information, but she understood why I was asking her about her life and agreed to talk about herself with my family on her first visit to our home in the fall of 1971.

Del was born June 9, 1912, on the Cattaraugus-Seneca Reservation, and she was a direct descendant of Tal-ga-yee-ta or Logan, Mingo Chief of the Cayuga Iroquois. She passed over on July 31, 1978 at the Onondaga Reservation, her home for almost her entire life.

Adelphina Logan, Onondaga
(Painting by David Wagner)

I believe Del was a member of the Eel Clan, although for some reason I cannot remember her ever mentioning this to me. However, she did give me her mother's Eel Clan spoon, which, by Iroquoian heredity rules, would make Del a member of this clan. She grew up in a log cabin on Onondaga Hill in Nedrow, New York. It was lined with cedar, and she could still remember the wonderful fragrance many years later. On one side of the family cabin was a big fireplace, and there was a loft where she used to keep her books. She always loved books and had some first editions of which she was very proud. Her family realized the benefits of education, so Del went to school on the reservation and then on to college—attending, at various times, Alfred, Syracuse, and Columbia Universities. Like Kee, she was well educated, and she also mentioned that, back then, an education like hers was rare for a man, even rarer for a woman, and practically unheard of for an Iroquois woman. Del became a member of the Alpha Phi sorority, and after college, a woman's educational honorary society, Delta Kappa Gamma.

With all of this "white man's education," as she put it, she was considered an expert by white people on her Native culture, and for this reason she was asked to be an advisor on Iroquois history for many organizations; but she confided on a number of occasions that her favorite place was always right here at the Indian Institute and with our family.

Like all her people when they were babies, when Del was very young, she was strapped to a guy-ho-sach or cradleboard. The word "cradleboard" was also used to identify the Jack-in-the-pulpit flower because it had the same hood to protect the flower that was present on Iroquois cradleboards to protect a baby. The Western world has something similar to the Iroquois cradleboard now, but it is not like Del's. Notice her cradleboard hanging on a longhouse sapling-support. It was in her family for generations and is the cradleboard onto which Del, her brother, and earlier ancestors had been strapped. In later life she gave it to us because she had no children to give it to, and we and the Institute were her family. Onondaga women knew a long time ago that a mother and child should be together as much as possible, hence the use of the cradleboard, which mother's usually wore on their backs and laid on the ground or hung from a tree near them when they were working. Their cradleboards were made with great care because they told the personal family history on the back, as Del describes in her book *Memories of Sweet Grass*:

> The Iroquois family was a close-knit unit. The children were and are looked on as the flower of family life, the seeds of the family's future. Propped in the fields or swinging gently from a tree branch, the child and the mother could watch each other, and when the time came, the cradleboard told the child his family history.
>
> Families traced their history on the back of the board. Near the bottom of the board was a clan and/or nation symbol—I was in the Snipe Clan, but our family tree started with the Deer Clan, and my people, the Onondaga Nation, are represented by a pine tree. ...Our families were always careful to identify ourselves in this fashion.
>
> Usually in the middle or near the middle is an ornamental line. From this main stem would be other lines like branches of a tree. These branches had likenesses of flowers on them, which represented the

number of daughters in that particular generation. On the same plane would be another line with representations of fruit. These indicated the number of sons in that generation. Thus, looking at each plane, a family could trace back a number of generations and the number of children—sons and daughters—in each [sort of like your family tree].

Somewhere, usually near the top, might be the symbol of the eagle. Indian legend tells us that the eagle was all-powerful and watched over all. With this ability and concern, the eagle was the medium for conveying prayers to the Creator. It symbolizes respect for the unknown.

Cradleboards were passed down to the eldest daughter, who then continued keeping the family record. If there were other daughters, they started their own family records.[13]

Adelphena Logan's Cradle Board

Del told me that the cradleboard for her and for all her people was "another daily reminder of a new life and of the Creator and the gifts we receive every minute of every day."

Notice her water drum resting on the lower of the two bunk-shelves along the left hand wall of the longhouse. As it was for Kee, this drum was important to Del at a very early age.

Music plays a major role in all aspects of northeastern American Indian society, and a water drum was the symbolic first gift Del received upon being born. The drum was constructed of a hollow or hollowed-out log with a bottom of wood and a deer or other animal hide stretched across its top. The drum was filled with water to various heights, depending upon the sound the owner desired to produce. Listen to the power of Del's words concerning her water drum. Listen to her poetic, almost hypnotic, way of talking. It is the magnificent voice of a superb Indian elder-teacher:

> A drum reminds us of our lives. My drum is old and full of memories, memories of things learned long ago, of my ancestors and of the ideas and accomplishments of my people and myself. Memories of sweet grass, the closeness of nature, the ancient and beautiful things of the woods. My drum is full of voices…of paddlers and their canoes…of lone people going through the trackless wilderness…of the far, far voices of singers…of dancers—their feathers keeping time with the beat. My drum speaks of olden times, for it is a diary of my people. It tells of brave and solemn chiefs seated around council fires; of powerful bodies representing strength, endurance, and stamina; of lofty spirits full of dreams, dreams of childhood and the future. My drum is a mingling of past, present, future. A treasured diary of my people is measured in the beat of my drum.[12]

Del went on to say: "We used this type [of water drum] because our songs have definite words. We sing words of our feelings and do not want just one monotonous note. By using the water drum we can pitch the instrument to the individual voice. A high voice requires little water in the drum, a deeper voice requires more water. Our singing, so tuned, is more pleasant to hear."[14]

Del made such a water drum for me, using a portion of a white birch trunk. She presented it to me in love, and I shall treasure it always, for she was welcoming me to her world.

Del was brought up in a traditional Iroquois way with all of the instruction and practice necessary for her to assume the role of an Iroquois wife and mother, perhaps even a clan leader and an elector of chiefs, as this was all part of her family tradition of a woman's service to her people. As a child, one of her first woman-jobs was to keep the family cabin clean. To sweep the floor she used a broom made of black ash—see it standing in the longhouse? For as long as she could remember, every family had one of these brooms. As with everything else, this object was much more than a broom.

> …we use them as a signal to tell a person we are not at home when the broom is across the door. When the broom is standing on the door frame, then it means "Come in, we will be right back." Sometimes there is no broom near the door or across the door; this leaves a question in the caller's mind....To this day our people never use the lock system or the police system, because everyone knows each other and we know the contents of our houses are the same. We do not have more than the other fellow. We have no man-made riches, as the only rich people among us are the ones who [serve the Creator and] have true and good friends.[15]

One of Del's other household tasks was making bark containers. Like Kee, at a very young age Del learned to make wooden and bark objects of the sort that you see on the longhouse floor. Her people still employed wood objects like these for personal use and traditional ceremonials at that time; later these were made largely to trade or sell to white people. However, when they were still young Del's Iroquois people and Kee's Ojibway had also adopted many of the white man's products to use in their kitchens, including pottery, china, forks, knives, spoons, iron and aluminum cooking pots and pans. In her book Del wrote:

> Some historians have made it appear that the Indians ate from a common pot. We had huge containers, as restaurants now do, for quantity cooking when large numbers gathered together, but we did not individually "dip into the pot." We would use a bark ladle, remove a portion to our individual bark bowl and eat with our individual spoon.
>
> Our people would obtain the bark during the time from the first or middle of May until the third week in June. During this period one can be fairly sure the tree will heal; at any other time the process is forced and the tree may be destroyed. Also at this time no staining is liable to occur. Any other time the bark is apt to stain.[16]

Del and her Onondaga family ate together, and as she put it, "We had good manners." A meal was a time for an Onondaga family to thank the Creator for the blessings of their food and their family. The Iroquois family would usually converse very little in the early stages of a meal for they wanted to give their full attention to the wonderful gift of the food they were eating. Only after the meal was over did any serious discussion take place, and this was true from a simple Iroquois family gathering to the most important Iroquois councils. When the family talked over meals, as they did at times, it was about pleasant or good things; they never talked about business or unpleasant things. This was considered rude, especially when guests were present.

The clothes Del wore from her childhood were mostly the same as the white woman's, although she and other Iroquois people still wore traditional dress for some of their special ceremonies. Many of the white-woman-style dresses she wore were special to her and to her people. According to Del:

> From the earliest period of white contact, cloth for making our own clothes was a very important trade

item. So important that when treaties were made between the United States government and the individual tribes, the treaty frequently stipulated that a yearly grant of cloth would go to the tribe to meet one of the practical needs of our people. A treaty ratified in 1794 with the United States saw the Iroquois ceding large tracts of land in the Ohio Valley to the United States, and, as part of this exchange, the Iroquois were to be paid in bolts of cloth. As time passed the government of the United States ceased to fulfill its promise to give bolts of cloth. Today the Iroquois people receive a small amount of yardage per person per year. It has become tradition for each family to make their family costumes from the treaty cloth.

The federal government is now asking that the Iroquois accept money instead of cloth for the 1794 Treaty. This is asked to ease the bookkeeping in the federal office. The Iroquois people feel that this token payment in cloth represents an obligation on the part of the United States government to keep its word. If payment in money were accepted by the Iroquois, according to our beliefs of honor in such dealings, the words of the treaty would be broken.[17]

Like Kee, as Del grew up, things didn't go well for her, trying, as she did, to live as an Indian in the white world. Despite the education and the other advantages she had, living where she did and with the type of family she grew up with, she observed and heard and read about many terrible experiences her people had suffered. At first there were the history lessons in school about such things as Sullivan's raids through their homeland—how his troops drove people from their villages, burned their food reserves for the winter, and left women and children to starve in the bitter cold. In her later years, every time Del thought of this particular story, she would become very upset. In fact, the only time I ever saw her really angry was when she somehow brought up the subject as an example of the white treatment of her people.

As I have previously mentioned, Del missed having children. She always loved them and worked with them for almost half of her life—thirty years—as Director of Arts and Crafts for the city of Syracuse Parks and Recreation Department. Del had children of every faith and color, and as a typical Iroquois mother, she loved them all. She confided that some of her happiest days were spent "with my kids," and later with our children, and that she was so proud of her title as a "grandmother" in our family.

Like Kee, Del recorded her thoughts for future generations to read. Her last book, *Memories of Sweet Grass,* was not only a death quest (as previously mentioned) but was special to her personally, for it reminded her of so many good memories of her childhood with her brother and her parents when they were able to live the Onondaga way, "without the interference of white folks," as she put it.

The worst single event in Del's life happened a few years before she met us. Some "white hoodlums," as she called them, came to her family cabin, which she still lived in by herself, and stole the precious family things she kept there. To hide what they had done, they burned her parents' home to the ground with her precious library inside. She had been filled with such a rage against white people. But then some friendly and thoughtful white people had come along, believing in her and her people's faith, and this had greatly affected her. She was "sadder and wiser," she said, after having come to grips with such a terrible tragedy, but she had wanted to continue her life-path as an educator for her own people, for the Creator, and for the "good white people like you" (meaning my family and some of us at the Indian Institute).

It is a great honor for me, at this time, to share with you stories about these two elders who have offered so much to me and countless others through their lives of teaching and service and through their contributions to the Institute. Let us now talk about a few major activities that so symbolize Kee's and Del's Creator-inspired faith.

Chapter 11

The Role of Tobacco and the Pipe for Religious and Ceremonial Purposes

According to the teachings of many Indian elders, one of the most important plants to Native Americans is native or unprocessed tobacco. It is used traditionally as a means of communicating with the Creator during religious and healing ceremonies and political and social events. Because of this all-important custom, tobacco has always been considered one of the most sacred plants by the northeastern American Indian people. Tobacco similar to the type grown today was found in the more southerly regions of our country. In colder locations, northern Algonquin Nations typically used a mixture of other plants for the same purposes. The Ojibway called this mixture kinnikinnick. Kinnikinnick was made of white cedar leaves dried and made into a powder, and then mixed with the leaves of pearly everlasting and bearberry. Other northeastern nations used different combinations of plants, including corn silk and leaves of the lobelia family, such as a low-growing plant called Indian tobacco. I find all of the tobaccos I have been offered at special Native ceremonies to be quite strong, and the tradition of not inhaling is most welcome.

The first of five uses of the tobacco plant that I wish to share is a practical one in which, traditionally, a shaman would scatter tobacco seeds in potential new locations for his village; if the seeds sprouted and grew, this was a sign of a Creator-blessed spot to settle. As long as the tobacco self-seeded and grew in the following years, this was where the people were meant to live and plant their crops. When the tobacco no longer sprouted in the spring, it was time for the village to move. As a believer in the Indian faith and as a scientist, I like this idea because it has both a traditional, religious side, and also practical ramifications. Broadcast seed, especially seeds of nutrient-hungry tobacco, will take root only on decent soil where other crops like the Iroquois Three Sisters—corn, beans, and squash—will grow luxuriantly as well. Yet even with the Indian's skilled practices, farming the fields around their village year after year cannot help but reduce the soil's fertility. This process of soil utilization to a point of the near exhaustion of the soil's key trace elements usually lasted about ten years or so. After the people left an area, the land was allowed to lie fallow and recover its fertility in a natural way for possible future use.

When establishing the Indian Institute traditional garden beside the replicated northeastern American Indian village, Native American staff scattered native tobacco in a small area of the potential garden site, and it flourished there for a number of years. During that time our staff grew beans, squash, and Indian flint corn, all planted in the traditional hill method.

Another use of tobacco is to scatter dried leaves into a small fire of dried twigs, mouse nests, or today dried sage leaves, so the smoke may spiral up to the Creator, and purify and bless everything here on Mother Earth from objects, such as a wolf totem-fetish to institutional ceremonies, such as those at the Indian Institute. Tobacco leaves are also offered to groups of people—at our wedding ceremony, for example—and at special ceremonies, such as sweat lodge healing services. At the end of a mourning period, the smoke of tobacco leaf is also used as a primary part of a shared remembrance service for a loved one who has passed over.

Equally beautiful is the tradition of placing a small amount of tobacco next to or in an object that is sacred because of the individual to whom it belonged. This is done as an offering of thanksgiving to the Creator for a person's life. As I have mentioned, the Maestro did this on his remarkable evening visit to our Institute when he deposited an offering of tobacco leaves in the cabinet drawer containing what was purported to be Sitting Bull's jacket.

Tobacco leaves are also smoked in a pipe. Notice on the lower bunk-shelf a pipe with its two parts—bowl and stem—separated. To the Ojibway people, the pipe bowl represents their Earth Mother and the wooden, hollowed-out pipe stem represents Father Man. The way the pipe is adorned and stored is indicative of the Indian way of reminding celebrants of the Creator's presence in all things and the potentially sacred nature of the pipe when it is used. Throughout much of the northern Midwest, the pipe bowl was traditionally made of red soapstone from Minnesota called katlonite, a relatively soft rock that is easily carved. Soapstone, clay, corncobs, wood, and other materials were often used for a pipe bowl, as well. The stem is adorned with such items as a leather thong to which a bird feather or feathers, an animal bone (often a deer toe bone), and a stone spear point or arrowhead are to be attached. These objects remind the pipe user of the human's role in the plant, animal, and mineral parts of the Creator's world. When the bowl and stem are joined, the pipe is energized with sacred powers for the intended services to be rendered.

Sacred pipes have two special uses. The first is for important ceremonies, such as religious rites, smudge and purification rituals, healing services, council meetings, and other significant ceremonial happenings. In any service calling for the use of a pipe, the dried leaves of Ojibway kinnikinnick (or the leaves of other plants traditionally used by northeastern American Indians) are crushed and packed tightly into the red pipe. Among the Ojibway, the pipe is employed principally during formal opening and closing ceremonies for political or religious meetings, where the host lights the pipe and then draws vigorously on it. While the smoke rises, he intones the proper prayers for the meeting, raising the pipe up to the Creator and then extending it to the east, south, west, north, and to Mother Earth. Then, if it is part of that particular ritual, the pipe is passed in a circle to the participants who will each offer a puff of smoke to the Creator.

The second use of these pipes is for social occasions and celebrations. In the Ojibway tradition a pipe was employed to welcome special guests to a home, village, or nation; to celebrate events like weddings; and for other similar purposes.

With the completion of the pipe ceremony, the pipe parts are separated. When not in use, the pipe is stored in two sections to prevent its power from being dissipated. The pipe is usually carefully wrapped in buck or doeskin, and is not reassembled until the next ceremonial occasion. The pipe is also generally protected and cared for by a specific clan within each Ojibway band.

Del has written eloquently about the meaning and use of pipes by Iroquoian people. Let me quote again from *Memories of Sweet Grass*:

> The pipe is common to all Indian people. In the old days to make smoke was to pray. Iroquois people never did this without reason. Tobacco was always offered to the Unknown Quantity [the Creator], for in the Unknown Quantity my people found thanksgiving for things bestowed. They knew these blessings came from one greater than the human mind could be. As incense is burned in some Christian churches during religious services today, so our people raised the smoke of the pipe to the four winds.
>
> The pipe, to our people, was supposed to be a living altar, with a head and body like a human being. The handle of the pipe symbolized the human spine; the bowl of the pipe, the head—the soul of the pipe. The piece that joins the handle to the pipe is the breath of the pipe.
>
> To offer the pipe was to offer communion. It was to establish a relationship between friends and enemies alike. The pipe was smoked by the principal men of the nations to seal a friendship. Thus came the term "peace pipe," although we used the pipe in other ceremonies, too.
>
> When our people got together, regardless of whether they were chiefs or not, a pipe was passed around to symbolize that the group was joined together to concentrate on the problem before them. The pipe signified meditation. We believe all life is a

circle, so that when the pipe was passed around and returned to the leader, it meant that each one was thinking on the problem. If...no one spoke, it signified that [all of the people were] still meditating and no one was ready to discuss the problem. The Council members would remain until the situation was carefully thought out and finally discussed.

In the old days no young man was allowed to use the tobacco in this form (smoked in a pipe) until he had become an accomplished adult. By this we mean, until he had done something for his family and for his community that was constructive. When this had been accomplished, the honor went to the family, not the individual.

A ceremony in which the pipe still has deep meaning is the Condolence Service. The ceremony is actually a eulogy, a recitation of all things that have passed down to our people through the generations. Now, instead of each person making his own pipe, the Council buys them. The little individual pipes are passed out after the greeting. We know this is going to happen, so we bring tobacco with us. The pipes, individually received, are marked for that particular occasion and kept as mementoes.[18]

Chapter 12

The Role of Games of Chance for Religious and Ceremonial Purposes

There is so much more to see and learn about in the longhouse. I called your attention to the dice and lacrosse stick as we first entered this room. These raise another important topic—the role of games of chance, called "gaming," in northeastern American Indian society.

Notice I use the word "gaming" and not "gambling," which today is exemplified by Indian and other people's casinos. Like so many other practices of Indian people, the process of gaming has been misinterpreted and misunderstood for many years by people without an Indian's perspective on this custom. Before the coming of the white man, traditional Iroquois games of chance were not only religious in origin and associated with their major seasonal holidays and other special occasions, but they were also conducted simply to win for the pride of a nation or a group within the nation, not for any personal gain.

Over time the Western influence has changed the northeastern American Indians' traditional purposes for gaming. It used to be among the Iroquois, for instance, that gaming was to decide who would win the opportunity to do all the work for religious ceremonies and to serve the "losers." A monetary reward was never a part of gaming. For many Native Americans, the traditional idea of gaming has changed over the years to the current practice of gambling for financial gain (for money). This has resulted in the Indians' ability to purchase many of the Western white world's "benefits," to be sure, but it has also resulted in their becoming part of the Western world's problematic standard of measuring an individual's success in life by their money, by how "rich" they are.

Trudie Lamb Richmond, our Schaghticoke staff member for a number of years, wrote an article for the Institute entitled "Games of Chance and Their Significance among Native Americans." She is knowledgeable not only about games Algonquin people participated in, but also about games the Iroquois people played.

Trudie Lamb Richmond, Schaghticoke
(Painting by David Wagner)

According to Trudie:

> Games occurred in great variety among Native American groups throughout the North American continent, but with one common thread: their religious or ceremonial significance....Although much information, particularly on peoples of the Northeast, has been deeply buried with the past, there is still much which can be obtained from these people who still practice their ancient traditions.

Indian games can be divided into two categories: games of chance and games of dexterity and skill. Games of skill include a variety of ball games like lacrosse and throwing a javelin (called a snow snake)...across the ice.

Gambling games are basically comprised of hand games, stick games, and bowl games.

The Iroquois explain that the Sacred Bowl Game, "Gus-ka'-eh", when played during the four day Mid-winter [festival], is not only meant to maintain a balance in nature, but also is meant to amuse those life-giving forces, to please the plant and animal world, and to make the Creator laugh. The players divide into two teams, determined by clans or moieties (a half of a group, the group being divided into two halves for social, political, recreational...purposes). The game opens with a gaming prayer that asks for good fortune, health, and happiness for the people, followed by a special game song that is expected to drive out evil spirits. Each clan concentrates on singing with one voice and one mind in order to bring luck over to its side.

The Iroquois Bowl Game consisted of six peach stones and a wooden tray. The stones or antler sections were burned or painted on one side and the other side left plain. The tray was used to toss the stones into the air. If five stones landed all of one color, this equaled one point; six stones all of one color equaled five points; and less than five stones of one color counted as zero.

Wagering was an integral part of all gambling games and greatly misunderstood by the Christian mind....It was a very difficult concept for the materialistic mind to grasp. None-the-less, everyone brought his or her best possession to be wagered, whether it was an article of clothing, special pair of moccasins, strings of wampum, [or] baskets of corn. The game could last several days. During Mid-winter it was the last two days of the ceremony. Many accounts read that the game continued until one side lost all but their breechclouts. By playing these games as an offering, it was believed that the "Patrons of Play" could be called upon to bring rain, ensure a rich harvest, remedy illness, and expel evil spirits....

A favorite sitting-down sport played by Woodland Indians was the moccasin guessing game. Although the game varied among the tribes, the basic idea was taking four moccasins and placing four objects, one of which was marked in some way, under the moccasins. Dividing into two teams, the leaders, previously selected for their skills in guessing, would determine which held the marked object....The one selected as leader of his clan or moiety was primarily chosen by what had been revealed or interpreted in his or her dream...for dreams played an important role.

The game was accompanied by drumming and great singing....Man played these guessing games knowing that there are many mysteries in life to which only the Creator holds the answer and winning is one of them. Hence, man willingly gambles for high stakes, emulating the early "Patrons of Play."

Unfortunately there is little vestige of any of the games of chance remaining in southern New England, as they were forbidden and outlawed by the colonists along with our dress, customs, and dance. As for the Iroquois, they view "Gus-ka'-eh" as a very important part of their ceremonies, and hold on to it very firmly, as something to be passed down to each new generation as part of their age-old tradition.[19]

Del Logan also talked with me on numerous occasions about the major role gaming and games of chance played in Iroquoian society. Their clans were divided into two moieties that took part in the games of skill and chance: the Longhouse people, who belonged to the forest animal clans, and the Mud House people, who belonged to the water animal clans.

Before Del's Onondaga people started any of their religious ceremonies, they had to determine who was going to have each duty. They did not have to call for volunteers because everyone wanted to help and it was an honor to do so. The best way they found was that one house, the Longhouse, played against the other house, the Mud House, for the privilege of serving in this way.

Notice the antler dice again, resting on a skin on a lower bunk-shelf. The Onondaga threw the little antler-section dice into the air and counted their points from the way the antler sections landed, as Trudie has just described. As with the Algonquin and the Iroquois, the object was to play to win and to work! The winning house did all the hosting, all the cooking, all of the serving—everything for that ceremony. The winners wore cornhusk masks in these services to indicated they were the "doers"; they participated in the services and notified different people in the village of various events that were going to happen and their religious meaning.

Northeastern American Indian faith is so beautiful to me because it pervades all aspects of normal living activities—even gaming has deep religious overtones. In addition to daily reminders of the Creator, special seasonal and other all-day ceremonies are held to acknowledge the relationship of the people to the Creator and the cycle of the seasons.

Chapter 13

Other Life Events and Ceremonies

The Algonquin and the Iroquois of the northeast both have major yearly celebrations—one for each season—that are conducted over a period of days by the entire village. Although these events involve many activities like feasting, dancing, and gaming, their main purpose is to give thanksgiving for all the Creator's blessings at that time of year.

The Onondaga and other Iroquois people employ words of thanksgiving for the opening and closing of all seasonal, religious, ceremonial, and governmental events. What is so special to me about this custom is that the tradition of the Thanksgiving Offerings continues to this very day. While the form of the prayers dates back over 1,000 years to "The Great Law of Peace" and a man called the Peacemaker, the person who is chosen to say the prayer finds their own words. This is in keeping with the personal and hence unique nature of northeastern American Indian faith, as I have mentioned earlier.

The Thanksgiving Offerings begin with an exhortation to the people to serve the Creator in balance and harmony with each other and with all living things. This is followed by salutations to Mother Earth, Water, the World, Fish, Plants, Food Plants, Medicinal Herbs, Animals, Trees, Birds, the Four Winds, Thunder Beings, the Sun, Grandmother Moon, the Stars, their elder-teachers, and, with the most profound and heartfelt thanksgiving, the Creator of their world. Each of these salutations is concluded with the same traditional invocation: "Now our minds are one."

Trudie Lamb explains the tradition this way:

> With the seasons moving in continuous cycles, it is clear that there is a balance of nature and a natural order of things. Native American people believe that they have a duty and an obligation to fulfill in maintaining that balance and natural order....They

believe that all living things were given instructions as to how to live in order not to work against the forces of nature. This is clearly reflected in the ceremonies, songs and dances that are closely related to many tribes of the Northeast. Many of these ceremonies were and are an integral part of the seasonal changes—e.g., Green Corn Ceremony, Strawberry Festival, Mid-winter Ceremony.

Here in the Northeast, especially among the Iroquois, the Mid-winter Ceremony is the most important to the people of the Longhouse. It plays an integral role in maintaining the balance of the forces of life. It is a time of thanksgiving for what has been given as well as prayers that the coming spring will bring continued life. It is a time of sacred ceremonies, special songs and dances. For the Longhouse people it is also a time for the reciting of the Thanksgiving Prayer....The Thanksgiving Prayer is recited to bring back the old order of things and is meant to give added strength to the ceremony....It is a time of thanksgiving for all that has been provided. And it is asked that the food prepared and stored will last through the winter cycle. It is asked that the coming spring will provide a good planting season. With the people being of one mind, it is believed that the Creator of all things will maintain the balance of the cycle of life and continue to provide sustenance as long as the earth shall endure.[20]

Kee and Del taught me that traditionally the Ojibway and the Onondaga had four major religious and social ceremonies every year to represent each of the four seasons. These events lasted up to five days, and in some cases even longer. While the names of these festivals of thanksgiving may be slightly different from nation to nation, the celebrations were held at approximately the same times and for the same reasons each year. The Ojibway and other northeastern Algonquin Nations celebrated the Mid-winter or Sugar Maple Festival (usually in late January or February); the "Bands Combining" with the melting of ice in the ponds and lakes, when food became more plentiful and the people could return to larger villages (usually in late March or April); the Harvest Festival (usually in August or September); and the "Bands Separating" (usually in November or December) before the Ojibway traditionally dispersed from larger summer villages to smaller, extended-family groups to make hunting and food gathering easier in the winter and early spring months.

According to Del Logan, the Onondaga Iroquois practiced the Harvest Festival in the fall and the Sugar Maple Festival in the Mid-winter, but they had lived in permanent villages for so long that they didn't practice the "Bands-Combining" or "Bands-Separating" Ceremonies. Instead, they celebrated the Strawberry Festival in the spring and the Green Corn Festival in the summer. As time has gone by, however, the types of ceremonies of the Iroquois and Algonquin Nations have become somewhat blurred. For instance, Algonquin Nations in our area may also practice the Strawberry and the Green Corn Festivals, but the great importance and meaning of these seasonal Iroquoian-type ceremonies has remained the same.

The Mid-winter or Sugar Maple Festival is a good illustration of the combination of the spiritual and practical ways northeastern American Indians approach their daily lives and their ceremonies. This festival is held when winter, with its short days and inherent hardships, seems to be never ending, and human spirits are at their lowest. For it is then that the first sign of warmer weather always occurs: the traditional mid-winter thaw. The resulting rise of sap in the maple trees is a signal that spring, with all its promise, will return soon. This is the perfect time for the people to have a big party celebrating the end of another winter. According to Del Logan, the Onondaga hold a lengthy holiday at this time of year centered on the religious rites of thanksgiving—thanking the Creator for providing the means for the group to survive another winter, for the precious gift of the harvest of maple sap, and for the opportunity for the people to celebrate, to feast, and to dance. But these prayers also stress the practical. For instance, the expression of special thanks to the Creator might be given for not allowing a tree limb to land on a dwelling during a fierce winter storm and hurt someone. The ceremony ends with great joy and the celebration of earthly pursuits: feasting, gaming, playing sports, music, and dancing.

The Harvest Festival is a universally practiced northeastern American Indian holiday. This one has become special to the Indian Institute because Del, as her gift to us when we were first starting to plan our museum, offered to come down with her Onondaga Iroquois extended family to Connecticut and share the prayers, chants, dances, and food of this important religious holiday. This festival represents, according to Del, the giving of life for the future. The service, shortened into a two-hour presentation for the Indian Institute visit, would normally last four days.

In Del's own words, the Harvest Festival is first and foremost a celebration of thanksgiving:

> The future would not be possible if the Creator did not give warm days, rain and good breezes. When we gather the harvest, we know that our humble prayers have been heard....This is a service of thanksgiving.
>
> In this Harvest Festival, we offer a great prayer chant to our Creator. We acknowledge our three sisters—beans, corn and squash....
>
> In perpetual humbleness we express gratitude for the harvest—without which we would be unable to live.
>
> We give humble thanks, too, for the health of our children; for our young mothers and fathers; and for the safe and secure wisdom of our elderly.
>
> ...and so we gather in dance, chant and song—as we shall for our friends in Washington [Connecticut].[21]

Before we move on to the next subject, northeastern American Indian ways of healing, it is my pleasure to invite you to attend one of these ceremonies at the Institute so that you may experience firsthand the power of the words and the actions of the northeastern and other Indian elder-leaders.

Chapter 14

The Indian Ways of Healing

Keewaydinoquay had a vast knowledge of the Ojibway medicinal uses of plants gained over a lifetime of study. She shared much with me, not about the healing rituals themselves, but about the whole process of healing and the plants that were involved.

The Ojibway approach to healing is a practical one, and it takes years of study to qualify an individual to do it properly. Since as far back as Ojibway memory of this practice goes, their elders have taught that a serious illness or physical injury should not be treated solely with medication, as we of the Western world are still inclined to do today. The treating doctor (called a medicine man, or in rarer cases, a medicine woman, like Kee) must treat the whole person—their soul-spirit-mind and their physical body. The doctor then becomes a vehicle for the Creator's Aura to occupy a part of the patient's aura in order to cure the mental part of the problem, and, if necessary, the medicine person will recommend appropriate plant medicines to treat the physical problem. This is because the Ojibway have long believed that all things are related and must be in harmony, including all parts of their body and soul-spirit, and that both areas must be treated for true healing to occur.

The Ojibway have several different practices and ceremonies for healing. They use special prayers to the Creator and to those involved to cure their sick. These prayer ceremonies can be carried out by a special individual or a group of individuals, and the person or persons for whom the prayers are offered may be present but it is not necessary. Do these really work? They do, indeed! Let me read several letters that I have received from people who have actually experienced this type of healing. The first is from Laurie (Mac Arthur) Harris, the widow of Irving "Ernie" Harris, former chief of the Schaghticoke

Indian Nation in Kent, Connecticut. The letter is dated October 24, 2004.

Dear Ned,

Thirty years ago September 27th, seven days after the birth of my fifth child, I hemorrhaged. After three operations, units of rare blood, sixteen days in intensive care, and later with peritonitis and pneumonia, I had been in a coma for two weeks. A dear friend, Tom Two Arrows, called and inquired for the family, as was the habit of all of our Indian friends.

My husband had been told by the doctors that my death was imminent, within the next day or two. He shared with Tom that I was dying. Tom told him he would gather friends outdoors at midnight, for there was a full harvest moon that very night, and they would smoke tobacco. If the smoke rose straight up, the evil spirits would leave my body. He explained this ritual could only be performed once.

At midnight I awoke and enquired of the nurse, was it a streetlight or the moon outside my window? She replied it was the full moon. I was pain free, totally rested, totally at peace.

Ernie arrived in the morning with the story of what Tom Two Arrows had done. We spent a wonderful day marveling at our gift.

I went on to raise five children and at forty-four years old became a nurse. Bringing peace to many, I was able to teach with a guarantee that people in a coma *can* hear, for I, and others can attest to this fact.

A couple of years later, my beloved father lay dying in the same hospital. I wrote to Two Arrows and asked him to pray for a peaceful death for my father. I explained to Tom that my father loved nature, hunted and fished with respect, knew plants and trees, and rescued countless wild creatures over the years.

Tom in his wisdom totally ignored me. He wrote my father and taped an aluminum foil packet to the letter containing tobacco seeds. He explained that my father would leave the hospital. He needed to plant those seeds in a place where he could see them. As they grew and flourished, so would his strength come back.

My father had a hospital bed beside a bay window. Outside was a small terrace and the seeds were planted there.

Sure enough he was sitting on the patio in the sun while his little garden grew and flourished. He lived to see another grandchild and died peacefully in his sleep.

I am so happy to have this chance to share my story. We were ordinary people, living ordinary lives, who were touched by an ancient and powerful force.

Thank you, Ned, for allowing me to share this story with others!

Laurie Ellen Mac Arthur Harris[22]

A second letter involves the cure of a very serious, potentially terminal cancer, this time with the use of tobacco leaf pouches. The letter was written by Maurice "Butch" Lydem, who was a cultural resource manager of the Schaghticoke Nation at the time. In the letter he talks about the Creator's gift of the tobacco plant and the power of the tobacco leaves. A pouch of unburned tobacco or the smoke of burned tobacco can become a link to the Creator and permit the healing process to commence for all kinds of illnesses and injuries. The letter reads:

> Dear Ned,
> Thank you for allowing me to share this very meaningful experience of mine with others.
> *The Power of the Spiritual Tobacco Pouch*
> There came a time about five years ago that I was diagnosed with stomach cancer and was scheduled for a major resection. My family got together and gave me an early Christmas Day with

everyone. We were all scared and nervous about the upcoming surgery but tried to have a good day.

It was a very cold day as I remember it—when a good friend, Trudie Lamb Richmond, came to the hospital to visit. She said she brought some spiritual tobacco bundles to help guide me through my recovery. She didn't know how many to make so she made many and told me I needed all the help that the Great Spirit could give me. She proceeded to put them all around me—at the top of the bed, on the side rails, and on the footboard. As she did this I felt a calmness come over me, and I knew a Power greater than mine was watching over me.

The nursing aides would come in—they would see all the red bundles hanging on all sides of the bed and would ask me what they were. I would explain that they were an offering to the Creator to hear my prayers and to help me on the path to recovery. I also explained that the position of the bundles represented the four winds, the four directions, and the four seasons. This went on for many days, and many visitors came to wish me well. On one particular day another aide came in and asked about the bundles. I said they were tobacco. She then replied, Oh, are you trying to quit smoking? I laid back and said, yes.

They just didn't understand what these meant to me and how much Power they had until one day a nun came in to visit. While visiting she noticed the red bundles and asked about them. I told her what they meant and how they lifted my spirit. She just stood there for a while, and this look came over her face. She said they represent the four winds, the four seasons, and the four directions! I said yes. Her response to me was, I can see why you feel that sacred Power. Do you realize that when you were admitted you came to the second floor room 202, you were then moved to room 211 and then to room 217? This took care of three directions, and your next move, my young man, will be going home to your family, safe and well. My prayers are also with you.

It's been over five years now, and I'm still cancer free thanks to my friend and the Creator. I live with His guidance every day.

Good luck and best wishes,

Maurice "Butch" Lydem[23]

Prayer-healing ceremonies can take place either in a hospital, as these were, or in a sweat lodge, a council room, the out-of-doors, a person's home, or another location where the patient or the practitioner is residing. Prayer ceremonies may also employ such additional items as medicinal plants, drums, tobacco pouches, a pipe filled with tobacco, a prayer wheel, or even a "cocktail" of potentially poisonous plants to induce in the healer x-ray vision and hallucinatory visions of what has caused the problem.

Note that there is no sweat lodge pictured in the mural to your right. This is because a sweat lodge is a holy place and should not be drawn or photographed for that reason. Traditional northeastern American Indians still use the sweat lodge and the hot steam produced in it for deeply religious experiences, as they have for hundreds of years. This is one of their major ways to communicate with the Creator. Sweat lodges are employed in a number of different ways—for an individual or a group, and for healing, doctoring, and purifying the body and the mind.

While I cannot share the religious ceremonial words themselves, for they are part of a sacred service, today so many people of different religious persuasions have experienced sweat lodge ceremonies that I feel I can share briefly now and in detail shortly the basic nature of the building and its purposes, including the basic steps of a healing or cleansing ceremony.

A sweat lodge of the northeastern American Indians is built in a low dome shape with a bent sapling frame of Grandmother Cedar poles, if possible, and covered with bark; or if it is a temporary structure, layers of canvas are used today. No light must be allowed to penetrate to the interior, except through a small, low, narrow door facing east, which is the entry and exit point and is tightly shut when the ceremonies are being held. In the center of the lodge, a round pit is dug. A series of red hot, glowing rocks are placed in this pit at appropriate times for the various ceremonies that are held there.

If the people taking part in the sweat lodge ceremony are not in harmony with the world around them or in the proper frame of mind, or if it is not the time for the person or loved one they represent to be healed in the Creator's view, they may not have the experience or results they seek. However, they are all cleansed and go out with clean minds and clean hearts to think things out anew, and to make new plans for the future. If the conditions of the environment and their minds and bodies are right, some of them, however, will be blessed with seeing and experiencing things of great import.

A drum can also be used in a healing ceremony. Del and I have already told you about the sacred nature of the water drum in Iroquois society. The drum plays a vital healing role in the lives of Ojibway people as well.

According to Kee, the drum of her people had been in the Ojibway Nation and in her band for over 300 years. This drum was used mainly for the purpose of healing. Apparently, each individual band of the Ojibway Nation has a drum, handed down over the years, and carefully treated and protected by a clan.

According to Kee, people over the years have risked their lives to protect this drum. During Kee's lifetime the drum was cared for by four people who watched it every minute. The drum was opened to Father Sun regularly and was used only for official functions. The Ojibway and fellow believers of other cultures offer blessed tobacco to it, and they still say prayers of thanksgiving when they think of this drum.

Ojibway and other northeastern American Indian nations usually augment the spiritual healing practices previously mentioned with local plants that they have learned over hundreds of years are useful for the physical and mental healing of all manner of illnesses. Many of their medicines have been cited in pharmaceutical journals and in a growing number of books about native plant uses. However, as I have mentioned earlier, pharmacological companies do very little research, overall, on North American Indian plant medicines, and apparently it is difficult to persuade people that no matter what the cost, our native plants are worthy of study for their potential to protect us against the host of new, creature-caused problems. On numerous occasions Kee told me she believed there was no disease or imbalance of any kind in the body that could not be healed through spiritual and plant-medicine power. She believed that for every human ailment the Creator had a plant cure. Today there are plant products that have been scientifically proven to treat or cure all manner of human ailments, ranging from heart and respiratory diseases to sores, ulcers, and uterine contractions. Why not AIDS and Parkinson's disease, the bird flu, the new flesh-eating bacteria, cancer, and on and on?

I have witnessed or participated in two additional northeastern Native American healing practices. The first involves tobacco leaf–filled pouches such as those used in Butch Lydem's cancer cure or a pipe filled with tobacco leaves to make a smoke offering to the Creator. Either way, the healer concludes this ceremony by offering the commonly used personal prayers asking for the Creator to do what is best for those involved in the current situation. The second healing practice involves a prayer wheel, a twelve-inch diameter (or larger) rim of wood covered with soft doe or buck skin with four thin spokes of twisted leather or other material radiating out from the center to represent the four directions. All the participants grip the wheel with their right hand. The healer stands in the east; the one to be healed stands in the west; and other participants may be similarly positioned in the south and north to complete and further empower the circle and the prayers of direction. I have heard of larger prayer wheels being used with more people involved, but I have never witnessed this.

As we discuss these ways of healing practiced by the Ojibway, I cannot help but think of "Turtle Woman." She was a rare friend who shared much with me about her life and her medical practice. In one memorable late night chat, she related her unusual service to her people, particularly as a young apprentice to the Midewewin. While under the influence of a cocktail of potentially lethal plants that was carefully administered and monitored by guardians, she could see extraordinary things. She made it very clear to me that the ceremony was an extremely dangerous one for the healer and that it could never be used for self-gain or pleasure. As a person who worked with plants in this way, she was honored by her people and treated with great respect. She and others who served were inducted into this way of curing at a very early age, and their life would be short, for the medication withered the liver and caused all manner of bodily injury. While under the influence of this mixture of plants, Turtle Woman's mind and senses were clear and supernaturally discerning, but her body was totally anesthetized. To protect her physical and mental wellbeing, she had to be carefully held up and watched at all times. Each subsequent time it did more damage to her system. Turtle Woman also described the process she went through to recover from this potentially fatal cocktail, but it took longer and longer with each use.

In order for Turtle Woman to engage in this type of vision-treatment, a supplicant had to follow a strict ritual. Her first case concerned a young, pregnant mother who was in labor and in severe distress. Under the effect of this medication, Turtle Woman was able to see with x-ray vision through the pregnant girl's abdominal wall and observe the problem: The umbilical cord was wrapped around the baby's neck preventing its birth. If not remedied immediately, the situation would soon result in the death of the child and perhaps the mother's as well. Turtle Woman was able to describe to the midwife what she saw and how to unwind the umbilical cord, and the mothers and the child's lives were saved.

Turtle Woman's last case was indicative, she said, of the cumulative effects of this plant mixture. With each dose she became more and more a part of the actual problem, and she had been warned by her teachers that after "X" number of cases (seven, as I remember)—which she was obligated to accept if she was asked in the traditional, ritualistic way—she would die in the process of this service. The last case she experienced frightened her, for she came so close to dying. As Turtle Woman described the event to me, a friend's husband had disappeared. Some years later, her friend met another man and they fell in love. But Michigan law at that time prevented her from marrying him because she was still legally married to the missing husband, whom she knew in her heart was dead. Turtle Woman was asked in the traditional way to help, and she did. She became the husband and retraced the route as he walked out into the woods toward a lake that fateful day some years before. Suddenly and unexpectedly he was set upon from behind, struck, and killed. Turtle Woman managed to fight her way back to full consciousness and note the location before she herself succumbed to the effect of the medication that she had taken by losing consciousness herself and dying as a result of experiencing the husband's death. Rather than report it to the local police, which she feared might lead to an investigation and potential exposure and harm to her society and herself, she reported the location to a hunter-friend. He subsequently went out hunting, found the bones where she had told him they would be, and reported the find to the police. The wife identified what was left of the clothing and other remains, and she was then legally able to marry the man she loved and begin a second life.

Turtle Woman shared with me her fear of being asked again to serve in this way, telling me she now saw too clearly her own demise with the next application; but, as she explained, few of her people still knew of the ceremonial way in which this help had to be solicited, and a number of years had already passed without such a request. I have not seen Turtle Woman since that time and recently learned that she has passed over. She was a great woman with much to share.

There is another interesting Ojibway and northeastern American Indian religious-based teaching that I have learned in the last thirty years from several Indian elders-healers. It concerns the Creator's potential role in the human search for our unique life-gift. The Creator may offer a series of "yellow caution lights"—my term, not an Indian one. Sickness and injuries may occur if a person has strayed too far from their appropriate life-path. I have personally experienced this and have also witnessed it in many others' lives since becoming aware of it. I have also observed that the yellow-caution-light consequences usually become more and more severe if a person does not "get the message" and change their life-direction. At last there is a red stoplight, a major setback that can be extremely serious. In general the symptoms of yellow light occurrences may disappear if one heeds them, but it has been my experience that if a red light is necessary, even with the redirection of one's life, the partial or more likely the total number of symptoms that were caused by this event do not disappear.

I wish at this time to relate one of the most dramatic yellow-light red-light series I have ever witnessed and in which I was actively involved. There was a young man in his early teens with a Creator-given gift of exceptional athletic ability. After a series of yellow lights—a broken wrist and other temporarily debilitating injuries in various sports in which he excelled—he was faced with the possibility of never walking again and needing a risky and pioneering operation on both ankles to offer any chance of recovery. In the process of dealing with this, he and I discussed his future and what message the Creator might be sending him. At that age it was difficult for this young man to see beyond his great love for sports. But in looking at himself over time, he began to realize that as special as this gift of athletic ability was, he had been granted another gift—an unusual talent for learning languages and a great interest in world cultures that later served him well in his career paths. In the meantime, visits to highly recommended orthopedic surgeons in Connecticut met with the same verdict: The operation was too risky and they would not perform it. However, the chief surgeon for two New York professional sports teams agreed to attempt an operation.

Shortly before the date of the operation, I attended a retreat in Rhinebeck, New York, for American Indian elder-teachers and other people from the northern hemisphere to explore the Old Way. Learning of this young man's problem, a group of Indian elders offered to pray for him in the appropriate way. They built a special wigwam-shaped, canvas-covered sweat lodge, similar to the one I described earlier, to hold a healing ceremony for this young man and others whom they had learned were suffering serious health issues as well.

On the day we hoped to have the healing ceremony, a severe thunderstorm with strong, almost hurricane-force winds literally shook the building that we were in. Our Native American leader, with vast experience in these ceremonies, promptly cancelled it—a wonderful lesson in itself. He explained that the time was clearly not right, and the natural order of things had to be obeyed. He added that to cancel the service did not mean that we had failed, for the powers of the Universe were so much greater than our own. When the harmony of our Earth Mother was upset, she could upset everything else—with hurricanes, earthquakes, tornados, floods, and winds like the one we had just experienced. It was a reminder that we always had to walk in balance with nature. We had to stay in the center, not go to extremes, or Mother Earth would then go to extremes to remind us of that.

The next sunrise promised a perfect midsummer morning—calm, sunny, and warm. The service was held late in the day and followed northeastern American Indian procedures with which I was familiar. Those who wished to participate, men and women, gathered in a beautiful woodland setting. They were requested to arrive early enough to sit or squat at a spot of their choosing on a cleared piece of ground behind the lodge, and to free their minds of negative thoughts. I prayed to the Creator, eyes closed, hands extended, palms upward, as was my custom, until I felt my mind was cleared of all worrisome and distracting thoughts and I began to experience a feeling of peace, contentment, and openness. Apparently several others could not achieve this state and therefore could not participate in the service. After I had cleared my mind as best I could, I stripped off my clothes down to my shorts (permissible on this day because some non-Indian men and women were participating) and wrapped a towel around me that I had been told to bring. The required offerings of tobacco that I was given, I scattered over nearby trees and an altar, which held a tobacco-filled pipe and was placed next to the door. I then crawled through the low opening of the eastern door, into the almost pitch-dark interior with the other participants. I became part of the outer circle of twenty-one people sitting against the outside wall; a second group of six formed an inner circle. All of us surrounded a central, recessed fire pit. We took our places, tightly packed together. When we were seated, our Native American leader called for outside helpers to pass six previously heated rocks one at a time into the lodge. These rocks were the size of one to two fists and red-hot. The leader and his assistant, kneeling on either side of the door, put them in the pit one by one after an offering of live cedar needles was dropped on each rock in turn to purify it. The first glowing rock represented our Earth Mother and was placed in the center of the pit. The second rock, placed as the first of a ring of rocks around the center one, represented the east and all that this direction meant to us. The third rock represented the south and the fourth, the west. The fifth represented the four seasons, and the sixth, carefully placed on top of the Earth Mother stone, was the grandfather of Creation. Then our leader asked us to join hands with the adults on either side of us to ensure that the power of the circle for healing that started with him would return to him. As I recall, it didn't. A person was recognized somehow and, after admitting that he was distracted, was excused. The circle was then deemed complete, and the first stage of the service began.

The door was sealed from the outside. The only light came from the fire and the glow of the heated stones. The leader sprinkled a mixture of water and cedar oil on them, producing a cloud of incense-steam and heat. We were instructed to stare at the stones, then shut our eyes, put ourselves at peace, see them in our mind's eye, and then free our spirit to fully participate in the ceremony.

Additional red-hot rocks were brought in at the beginning of the second and third stages. Each stage began when water and incense were thrown on these stones, making dense clouds of hot, scented fog that produced considerably more heat than the previous stage; and each ended with traditional chants and a drum roll.

At the end of the second stage and before the door was sealed again, water from Mother Earth was passed around to remind our group that we needed to replenish ourselves.

By late in the third stage, when the heat was extraordinarily intense, all pretense of modesty had vanished, towels were dropped, and I and the others were totally caught up in the feeling of closeness and sharing and the bond of energy we were experiencing through our handholding-circle.

At the end of the third stage, a previously prepared pipe on the altar just outside the door was passed in to our leader, who offered the pipe and the smoke it produced to the six directions. He then passed it around so the others could draw and release a ceremonial puff of their own with their personal prayers to the Creator before passing it on to the next individual. The last individual to receive the pipe, the assistant leader on the other side of the door, finished the tobacco, and the pipe was removed and taken apart before the doors were once again sealed for the fourth and hottest round.

As instructed, I closed my eyes and offered myself and the heat-related pain I was experiencing to my person in need, and, suddenly I had broken through the heat and the pain, and I felt nothing except elation! The time to pray for those specific people to be healed had come. During this process I found myself suspended in the air and looking down with others at the top of the intact sweat lodge. I turned to the gentleman on my right, who somehow was still holding my hand and who was floating next to me. I shall never forget my words or his. "Something has happened," I said, to which he replied, "I guess it has."

The ceremony continued for perhaps three-quarters of an hour. It ended with a final drum roll and chants, and the door was opened for the last time. I crawled out with the others in reverse order, offering prayers of thanksgiving in the doorway. We sat on the ground to cool off, drank lots of herbal water as recommended by our leaders, and put on our clothes. Before I left I shared my experience with one of the leaders, who said my vision was very special and boded well for my personal prayers. Others he had known had had similar experiences in the past. As I returned to my quarters I felt as if I could fly and that my feet seemed to barely touch the ground. The long-remembered association of my northern Wisconsin days with the smell of burning cedar and the extraordinary feeling of cleansing and newly found energy from the impact of the sweat lodge ceremony were overwhelming. I was filled with a sense of purity, wellbeing, and euphoria that I have never experienced other than after a sweat lodge.

I was also left with the clear awareness that the ceremony had indeed "worked." For whatever the reason, if there is an earthly one, I knew it had!

I returned from the retreat and, within a week, accompanied the young man to the hospital for the scheduled operation. New x-rays were requested and taken by the hospital before the operation was to be performed. They revealed that one leg had been completely healed, but that the other had only partially healed and would need a modified, less severe operation. Following the surgery, after a long and painful period of recuperation, the young man was able to walk again. Though he never regained the normal use of the still-affected ankle or regained his original level of performance, he played college sports and even ran in several marathons with considerable success.

Probably the most common healing ceremony of all is offering prayers wherever and whenever necessary. When Ojibway healers do this, they first purify themselves and then rub their palms together until they feel energy between them. Only then are they able to offer prayers for a person in need or, if possible, go to call on that person. In either case, they stand, palms up, in silent prayer, their energy now released to join the energy of the Creator. They then pray that the Creator grant what is best for the patient at that time in their life-path and share this prayer with the patient and their loved ones who may be present.

Given my physical problems and difficulty traveling, most of my healing efforts and a great deal of my religious life are carried out through this daily prayer-conversation (as many as ten to fifteen times a day, and sometimes more) with the Creator in the traditional northeastern Native American Way. These daily prayers take many forms. There are prayers of gratitude for a special gift from the Creator, such as a new day of life for others or for myself, or for the presence of a dear spouse, family, or friends in their life or mine. I also offer petitions for such items as an answer to a plea on someone else's or my behalf, or for the outcome of some imminent or future event—such as someone's potentially serious problem ending with a good medical report, or a bad accident resulting in a good prognosis for recovery. At the end of every prayer of petition, I have been taught to say "if it is Your Will." To me it is essential to acknowledge that it is not my will but the Creator's that defines the answer to my requests, as well intentioned as they may be.

A personal example that illustrates this Creator-inspired human healing power concerns our "daughter" Karen, who "adopted" our family as a teenager. A large tumor had grown almost overnight on the membrane of her uterus. A biopsy showed the presence of a small but significant number of pre-cancerous cells, not a good sign. In her forties, she was brought up in the Catholic tradition, was married and the mother of a young son. She had much to live for and many things she wished to do. She called us as she regularly does, and I immediately shared my faith in the Creator's Will, in the power of prayer, and in the Indian method of praying. I shared this Indian Way with her myself. She began this prayer-therapy with a sense of doubt, but after a short while she began to feel better, more relaxed, and more hopeful. She told me later that on the day of her operation she felt at peace and extremely confident that everything would be all right. Soon after the surgery we heard the glorious news: The tumor was encapsulated and benign, but pre-cancerous cells were present, and it was removed just in time. No further treatment of any kind was necessary. In her prayers Karen had requested that if she still had important tasks to be done for the Creator, including the raising of her son, that she be allowed the privilege of continuing her life-path. She has been healed, is with her growing son, and during the hurricane Katrina crisis felt the call to serve the Creator in a new and special way, to volunteer her services to the Red Cross for disaster relief. As a very kind and sweet person working in a pharmacy for some years, she felt she had special gifts to offer in this area, and she does.

Healing can also take place over time, after a person has largely given up attempting, unsuccessfully, to deal with a deep mental or physical problem through their own and others' prayers. The person involved must eventually realize or be counseled to let the Power of the Great Spirit and their aura take over their failed personal efforts. Let me relate a terrible event that followed this path in Kee's life. Her own words illustrate the power of this healing process:

> When I was young I was paddling across a big lake. I capsized in the rough water, died, and was resuscitated. Shortly thereafter, I lived with a man for five years. He left one day and never returned, leaving me with a baby girl. Soon after this, a social worker in Michigan came with a sheriff and took my little girl away from me "because we did not have separate bedrooms." I was devastated. Then I had an inspiration. I would get a white man's education so that I could become a social worker and have the evil power this white woman had. This was a terrible thing for me to do, and I did not follow up on it. Instead, I began teaching school, where, because of my Ojibway heritage, I treated all children with love. Twenty-five years later, while teaching in a very small school way up in northern Michigan, I found my daughter teaching in the same school! Truly I am sure this happened because I had given up trying to deal with the problem myself; I allowed the Great Spirit's Aura and my new sun-path to act, free of my own personal pig-headedness and hang-ups, to resolve this issue for me.[24]

During my later years I have been blessed to witness a number of cures as they occur through my and other's petitions to the Creator. I have seen everything ranging from the alleviation of pain to the change in direction of potentially serious illnesses, and from instant cures, to a sense of tranquility as the last hours of life approach. I have continued to see loved ones pass over, despite my every effort on their behalf, but I realize this is the Creator's Will, and I, fallible human being that I am, now accept this with a growing equanimity and deep sense of thanksgiving for the person's life and all that they have done for so many people while here on Mother Earth.

The act of healing, in and of itself, is a supreme gift from the Creator. The ability of one person, through the Creator, to serve others—to somehow help to relieve them of earthly sorrow, sickness, and pain, or to offer them a sense of peace and a possible new direction—is a precious life-task. But my involvement in this service has brought me an additional gift: the blessing of a frequent, close, and comfortable relationship with the Creator in doing this. What greater gift can a human being have than this?

Chapter 15

The Creator's Guidance through Visions

Ojibway people have found that the most revealing way to learn about their sun-path is to be blessed by the Creator with a vision or a series of visions. There are two ways by which a person can receive such a vision. The first is an overwhelming "aha" experience—particularly effective during the waking hours, but it happens during sleep as well. A complete surprise, neither expected nor sought by the person involved, it is granted by the Creator as a means of offering a new direction for the person's life-journey. This is the type of vision I was granted, which led to creating the Indian Institute. But this type of vision is rare, and because a vision still is so essential, particularly to a man's future sun-path, Ojibway and other northeastern American Indians believe that men must actively pursue a second way as well.

This second way traditionally begins early in life, with a very specific, four-day "vision quest" by boys, usually at the age of twelve or thereabouts. It takes place after a long and difficult period of preparation, including such possible activities as a major big-game hunting success (like killing a bear with a knife), physical hardships, fasting, and purification (usually involving a sweat lodge ceremony). The boy seeking a vision proceeds alone to an isolated location where spirits might reside, such as a clearing in the forest, a hilltop, or a place near water. Here the boy stays for a prescribed number of days. He remains largely immobile, usually fasting, meditating, praying, and even inflicting personal wounds on himself until a vision comes. After several days, if he is not fortunate enough to receive one, a leader comes to check on him. If he is having serious physical problems, the leader would make him stop before he could hurt himself badly, for every life has always been precious to northeastern American Indian people.

Traditionally, if a boy, or even a man in later life, was blessed by being given a vision in this way by the Creator, he was often beckoned by a spirit-figure. This figure led the boy, leaving his physical body behind, on a journey into the spirit world. It was in this spirit world that the boy acquired "spirit-guardian-helpers" and learned from them the future direction that his life should take and gained the power to implement this mission. In addition, the boy was informed of the appropriate objects—artifacts, stones, feathers, fur, etc.—from special parts of his life to put in a "medicine bundle," a leather pouch, which he often wore attached to his waist. In the spirit world he was also taught an appropriate dance and song to represent his vision. The successful vision seeker, now knowing the direction of his life-path, was transformed from a child with child's thoughts to the position of a secure and powerful adult. Traditionally, a vision could only be shared with a medicine man, to ensure its power, which might be lost if revealed or unheeded. Those so fortunate as to have a vision were honored with ceremonies, prayers, dancing, and feasting upon their return.

Women may also receive such vision-gifts, but these do not have the importance that they do for men, because the Creator has already given the supreme, primary gift to a woman: the ability to give new life.

To me personally, a vision, whether sought or unsolicited, has long been the key to my life-path. For those of us who are immersed in Western culture, the idea of a vision is hard to imagine because we have learned to be suspicious of the reality of this type of experience. We are also uncomfortable with the degree of silence and introspection that we think this demands of us, and are impatient with the suspected inactivity and contemplation we suppose must be required. These notions of silence, introspection, inactivity, and contemplation are suspect because many people do not consider them virtues in our Western culture. Rather, sloth or non-activity is considered inherently bad, and silence is thought to be a show of weakness exemplifying a lack of confidence and intelligence. Fortunately, to my way of thinking, I feel that the current growth in popularity of such disciplines as meditation and yoga has begun to change this perspective, and the importance of occasional, if not regular periods of contemplation and silence is a much more accepted practice in today's Western world. To me it is a way of seeing and learning new things about our world and ourselves. This can be extremely important in our life-long search for our unique capabilities and our Creator-inspired role in this earthly existence.

For example, my whole adult life has been a search, knowingly and, yes, often unknowingly, for what I am meant to do now and occasionally suggestions of what I am meant to do in the future—in other words how I am meant to serve the Creator on an ongoing basis. The older and more disabled I get, the more intent I am at discovering, undertaking, and finishing my remaining life-works while I still can— before it is my time to pass over. Now, at this late stage in my life, I am much more aware of the world around me. I have become convinced by the evolution of my life that every event has potential purpose and that every person I meet, I meet for a reason. The truth of this feeling has been borne out with incredible regularity by current "happenings." Even the hint of visions and vision-like experiences are extra special to me. They allow me to free myself from the confines of my physical infirmities and to soar to higher levels of awareness of events and situations that I may never have been a part of in any other way.

I do depart from the traditional restriction of telling only one special person about my vision and vision-like directions. I have always shared them with others. This is because I have found and therefore believe that these shared experiences somehow are all the more powerful and effective in our Western world of non-belief and lack of understanding. They are events that I hope have introduced others to a new way of thinking about a spirit-world and, at the very least, have introduced them to the reality of such a world in another's experience. Up to now the sharing of my not-infrequent visions has apparently not hurt but has enhanced them as far as I can see from my limited perspective here on Earth.

I have been taught that the two types of visions I have mentioned can come in three different ways: while one is awake, asleep (through dream messages and messengers), or over a considerable period of time (as a slow build up of interest in a life-direction finally reaching a total and sudden awareness of its potential for that person).

The first, which occurs while we are awake, can be a sudden and vivid image, or it can be the longer, spirit-led journey to a vision. The other two are less immediate but equally as effective when the meaning is fully recognized.

Having a vision is a profound experience that comes with great potential responsibility. First, a person must realize what the vision's message truly means. Next, they must not only be willing to act on it, no matter what the cost may appear to be to their current life, but they must also be true to this vision at all times, and this is not always as simple as it may sound. An example—and probably the most difficult life-path decision I have ever had to make—came in the form of an offer that was perhaps the single greatest honor I have ever received from one of my elder-teachers. After many personal discussions in which we shared our innermost dreams of earthly service, Keewaydinoquay invited me, as a kindred soul, to come live with her on an island in Lake Michigan for at least one year for the purpose of passing on to me her vast knowledge of medicinal plants. From my personal perspective, Kee was clearly aging at the time and in questionable health, and this appeared to be the right time to fulfill her commitment to leave for posterity her invaluable acquired wisdom on the subject, an undertaking she had never seriously considered until a personal awakening to this need at this current late stage in her life.

During the time Kee gave me to think about and discuss this offer with my wife, I received no direction of any kind from the Creator or from any other source, as I had prayed for and hoped. As hard as this decision was to make, I had to assume I was meant to stay, for some as yet unrealized reason, to serve the Institute I had co-founded and to remain with my family. After great thought and a number of discussions with my wife, I felt obligated to decline this honor.

That I made the right decision, however, was soon evident. Had I left for the year, the Indian Institute might well have undergone a serious financial crisis that I would not have been available to help meet. Because I stayed, I was present to participate in another truly miraculous event.

This "other worldly" experience began at the annual Washington Green Fair in July of 1987. I was wandering around, as one does at such events, when I noticed an older man, an elder, dressed in Indian garb and obviously a bit disoriented. I approached him to ask if I could help. He told me he was looking for a man named "Ned or Ed something" and an Indian museum somewhere in the area that was having financial difficulty. I said I was Ned Swigart, and, yes, our museum was having considerable financial difficulty at the time. I asked him how he knew this. He said only that he knew and that he had an unusual gift of being able to pray for money, which would then appear for Creator-inspired projects. He also told me he had a rough idea of where to come, but little else. He was of the Potawatomi Nation and lived on a small, largely uninhabited Island in Lake Michigan, as Kee did. He gave me his name but made me pledge I would never share it with anyone, or he might lose this gift. Of course, I did give my word, and would you believe, at this time in my life, his is the only Native American elder-teacher's name that I have forgotten. As I drove him the short distance to the Institute, he asked me how much money we needed at the moment to meet our financial obligations. I answered $100,000—not really a significant sum to larger, older institutions, but a huge sum to us at this early date in the Institute's existence and given the immediacy of its due date. I needed $40,000 right away to meet our payroll and loan payments. If that amount were covered, I could undoubtedly raise the additional $60,000 over the next several months to free the Institute from all immediate debt, something our board and finance committee felt strongly about. So we prayed in the Old Way that I was familiar with. Using a small smudge pot and untreated tobacco, he led the prayers, first of purification to enable us to approach the Creator, and then of thanksgiving to the Creator for the Institute and its work. He then mentioned the Institute's financial problems and the immediate need for $40,000 in cash. After only a few minutes, he concluded the prayers in the traditional way, looked up, and said, "You will have the money in four days."

He then requested that I take him to the nearest bus stop. The brevity of this ceremony took me by surprise. I asked if he would like to spend the night, and didn't he have something else he would like to do while he was here? He said no, this was it. I was amazed. He had come approximately 550 miles to pray for less than five minutes and then return to his island. I cannot imagine how he had discovered his special life-path gift, especially living in the isolated place that he did, but having found it, he obviously went to extreme lengths to practice it; and I have never known or heard about another living soul who possessed such a unique life-path service and practiced it as he did. In the car for the twenty-minute drive to the nearest bus stop, I asked him how I would get in touch with him to tell him how we had fared. He told me I couldn't. There were no telephones on the island. He would have to call me when he got to the dock where the ferry to his island was located. In the next day or so, I received an anonymous, unsolicited gift of $5,000, and by the fourth day the total of new monies was approximately $40,000! He called me late that day from the ferry dock phone as he had promised; it had taken him that long—four days—to get there by whatever means of transportation he had used. I thanked him profusely and said we had made the $40,000 goal. His terse answer was one I will never forget: "I thought so. Goodbye."

I never heard from him again.

My elder-teachers say visions can also come in one's dreams. I have studied at length and have practiced dream analysis for many years. Also, since this is one of his major life-gifts, I have learned a great deal from my Aztec elder-teacher, the Maestro, about this subject. He related to me that the world of dreams is another dimension of life as we know it. When we are awake we cannot fly, go to Mars, be in Africa one moment and in Alaska the next, or do a number of other wished-for activities well, such as skating, swimming, or playing baseball, that we have not been granted the talent to do in waking life. But in dreams we can participate in anything we may want to—for a door or a window to another dimension of existence has opened for us. We can go backward (I have experienced this with dramatic results) or forward in time, visit towns we have never been to, and meet people whom we have never met before. Days or years later we may drive through the town or see the person and know we have "been there" and "done that"—what I believe we call a "déjà vu" experience. For instance I traveled through a town in Wisconsin in a dream, and then later on when I drove through that town, I knew the way and even what was around the next corner. Also, of course, Del, Kee, and others have visited me in "dreams" to advise me on matters of immediate importance (perhaps I was dreaming, perhaps not).

Today many people have lost the knowledge of how to interpret dreams. Many dreams are common and personal, relating to the day's events or occurring when a person is unwell or has eaten too much; but there is still a message. Other dreams are very personal or very strange, and they may be of great meaning. Insights like this, at the most appropriate times, are truly among the Great Spirit's special gifts.

A dream, to my way of thinking, is just as potentially meaningful as a revelation while we are awake, but at times a dream-vision can have confusing imagery and even take on some of the characteristics of our normal, nightly dream-experience. For me, this type of dream-vision of what I should be doing in and with my life has been quite common when compared to only a very few visions when I have been awake. For example, after I retired from the Indian Institute in 1989, I fully intended to write a novel attempting to express my difficulties living between two worlds, the Western culture I was immersed in and the Indian Old Way, which I found to be personally more and more fulfilling and valuable as I grew older. I planned to articulate this via two main characters: a young man with a white father and a Mohawk mother who grew up on the St. Regis Mohawk Reservation and primarily followed his Indian heritage, and a young woman with a white father and a Cherokee mother who grew up in the white world and tried to follow her white inheritance. To write this novel, I went through my usual workday routine. I arose at 6:30am, had breakfast, showered, dressed, and at 8:00am, the time I had traditionally begun my day's work, came into my office to write on my computer.

Nothing happened.

This went on for almost a year—the most frustrating time that I believe I have ever experienced.

Then I had an extraordinary dream. In it I was a young man again with my Indian friends, freely living the traditional way, on "Indian Time"—when the moment was right rather than by any specific schedule—fishing and playing and free of all time constraints. The message was somehow crystal clear. No time clock. No daily routine. I was destined to write as I was meant to live and to think: when the Creator's Spirit moved me. I wrote, sometimes for hours, sometimes for abbreviated lengths of time, and at all times of the day and night. I also quickly realized that if this project was meant to be, the novel had to develop a life of its own on a level far beyond my limited abilities. I regularly ran into Indian concepts—like the overwhelming sense of stewardship and responsibility to "the People" that an Ojibway man must face for his whole life—that did not have words in English to describe them. At such times the budding novel would grind to a complete halt, and then another dream or insight would follow— sometimes nights or days later - with an example of how to express the concept in Western words and images.

The book has never been published, but I am now more than content with the result. This first book has been written and, with revisions based on what I have learned during the process and since I wrote it, may still be published at some future time *if* it is the Creator's Will, but this is academic at this point. In the meantime it is now apparent to me that it was meant to be a stepping stone to this presentation on northeastern American Indian faith because I learned so much about myself, the parameters of how I must write, and the inspiration and support provided by the Creator in the whole process.

A third type of vision-related experience is the most difficult to recognize but is probably the most common. It first takes the form of a series of suggestions concerning a potentially important, new life-path direction. These occur with increasing clarity and frequency over an extended period of time, until the vision-direction is so clear and powerful it leaves the person wondering how it had not been recognized earlier.

For instance, I graduated in 1950 from the Hotchkiss School, and the last thing I ever wanted to do was to be a teacher, and especially in a place as demanding, confining, and archaic as a boarding school. When I received my graduate diploma from the Yale School of Conservation in 1956, I found jobs in the conservation field were almost non-existent because the field was so new. A good friend, the director of a national conservation organization, advised me to consider teaching in a boarding school while waiting for an appropriate position. He suggested this would provide excellent preparation. I followed this suggestion but have never quite understood why this was so. The Gunnery School in Washington, Connecticut, immediately offered a position that appealed to me. Over the next three years I became increasingly aware that I was developing into a good teacher, somehow able to communicate with more and more students. I found I was really enjoying my work and especially my contacts with teenage boys (for The Gunnery was an all-boys school at the time).

At the end of three years of teaching, two important events occurred: The Gunnery senior class dedicated their yearbook to me, the highest honor a teacher may receive from the students at that school; and as my friend suggested, a wide variety of jobs in the field of conservation did, in fact, develop. It was decision time for my wife and me. Two diverging life-paths beckoned to us. The first was the path of my current career. The second was a path in a new-old direction, which I had always been interested in and was uniquely well qualified to pursue: the field of conservation. My wife and I agreed that if I was ever to find out whether conservation rather than teaching was my chosen field, now was the opportunity. We had no children as yet and were still young and adaptable. I accepted the offer that interested me the most, a pioneer position establishing educational programs and clubs to sponsor them in different geographical areas for the Massachusetts Audubon Society. However, after only one year, my wife and I realized I was satisfied but not happy in my conservation job, as successful as my efforts had been. On the other hand, it was quite obvious (the "aha" experience, at last) that I missed the students and teaching very much. Thus, in a period of six years, I had gone from not wanting to be a teacher to being ready to welcome without reservation this future career as a continuation of my life-path to serve the Creator.

My wife and I returned to Washington, and I spent the next twenty years (retiring in 1979 to move to the Indian Institute full time) doing extremely rewarding work at the school. I was now fully aware I indeed had had a very unusual life, quite unique actually, to bring to the classroom: my northeastern American Indian experience, my knowledge of the out-of-doors, and my graduate school training in conservation. My focus during these later years at the Gunnery School was increasingly centered on passing on to my students an understanding of our world and how to live in harmony with it. To that end, as my years of service at the school progressed, I was able to establish courses in ecology, archaeological field studies, and anthropological readings about Indian prehistory and history. I was also placed in charge of various extracurricular clubs and activities, including an outdoor club (a sports option) that I used to teach Indian ways of living and surviving in the outdoors.

If there is one lesson that I have learned during my lifetime, it is that a person's unique life gifts can lead them on a number of successfully completed, different paths during their lifetime and that a person is never too old to serve the Creator and undertake a new challenge that is Creator inspired.

Unfortunately, in a "modern life" of frenetic activity during every waking minute of every day, little time is available to be open and focused long enough for a thought, much less a vision, to find a way to express itself. I have experienced this. My life was too frantic and too fragmented during my early years of rearing a family and developing my careers to allow much introspection, as aware as I was of its importance in learning about my Creator-inspired life-path. However, I was indeed blessed that the vision-event to create the Indian Institute was still able to burst through my daily distraction during this period of my life. I also had the advantage over time of Ojibway and northeastern American Indian elder-teachers who, during my later years, were constantly offering me guidance on their way of living. Thus I became increasingly aware of the potential problem of becoming overwhelmed with distracting activities, and I learned to force myself to set aside necessarily brief but meaningful times during the day for introspection, for example, when I woke up in the morning, walked to work, went to bed, took a break away from the computer, drove anywhere alone, or waited for someone. At such times I would try to clear my mind of all the clutter of the day and let it just be open, blank, to possibly receive some precious suggestions about my life-path. This worked for me.

Try this idea of quiet times throughout the day, and if a new idea does get your attention, be aware that you face an immediate decision. Are you prepared to recognize it for what it might be—a thought of potential future importance? What follows is the hardest part of all, to accept the thought as worth considering, even if it does not seem of interest to you at that moment and goes against everything you believe you should do. As I have mentioned, the creation of the Indian Institute was just this for me, especially when I had already become a good teacher and enjoyed that profession. As I have also mentioned, everybody advised me that I was crazy to leave a promising career to follow this vision, for it could have been, and many predicted it would be, a disaster, but the Creator had assured me in my vision everything would be all right.

Think on this. The ability to have various visions that help to guide and maintain our lives along productive paths based on our unique abilities is a Creator-granted gift of immense value. Helpful visions are not rare, particularly the ones that occur in dreams or during the day in a moment of quiet time. I pray that you will recognize them for what they are, think about them, and benefit from all they may promise.

And as you do this, remember this longhouse classroom and the many suggestions it offers for how you too might live in harmony with Mother Earth and become a steward of our precious land.

We've come to the end of our walk through the Institute exhibit rooms. As we retrace our steps, I would like to share with you the three most important events that help define a northeastern American Indian's life in every way. Two are certainties in all of our lives: birth and passing over. The third is a key ingredient of how Indian and most other societies define their culture and the continuity of their nation or country: the wedding ceremony.

Chapter 16

The Birthing Ceremony

According to Keewaydinoquay, birth and passing over are the two most important events of her people, marking the beginning and the ending of the circle of life here on Earth. Ojibway family members participate in the birthing process with joy and thanksgiving. While the practices are still followed to some degree by Ojibway people in rural regions, modern Western ways are now commonly used, especially in urban and suburban areas, or when a hospital or medical care facility is available to the mother-to-be.

As we've mentioned, girls were traditionally taught that bearing a child was a privilege and a service to the village and the nation, and was supposed to be carried out calmly and with dignity as a natural part of a woman's life-path. The pain associated with the gift of giving birth was to be accepted stoically. Young women were also instructed on the best positions for birthing. While they were young and playing house, girls practiced with a "birthing bar," which I will define shortly, and learned the drum dances played during childbearing. From the time a daughter was very small, she was also given increasing responsibilities to serve her family and her community: everything from working around the wigwam, helping to carry the family baby, carrying bundles, assisting in the harvesting of food—all the normal daily activities that kept women in good physical shape. All of this training helped her when it came time to give birth.

As the birth of an Ojibway baby approached, by tradition, the baby's father usually built a special, small, birthing house of wigwam shape and construction, using white cedar, if possible. This special wigwam was located somewhat apart from the village and near water. No covering was put on the roof; only the frame was present so the mother could look up at the universe. When the young woman began labor, she went to this dwelling, and all her female relatives accompanied her. In the center of the floor was a pit a foot deep and usually lined with sweet and bracken fern right before the mother-to-be and her family arrived. Across this pit was placed a pole that served as a birthing bar. When the mother-to-be came in, she knelt or squatted in the pit and took a firm grip on the pole. Her female relatives started to pray to the Creator, while outside the wigwam an older man began to play various rhythms on a drum—all this according to the midwife's instructions as she watched and guided the mother-to-be in the birthing process. The other women danced to the different rhythms of the drum.

Being upright, moving rhythmically up and down to the sounds of the drum, recognizing the Creator's support, relaxing, and using the natural force of gravity aided the birthing process; and the traditional Ojibway birth was natural and usually swift, involving far less discomfort and pain than is associated with the modern Western-style of childbirth.

By Ojibway tradition, it was very important in the birthing process that the future mother accept whatever pain she might experience as a holy offering for her people, and not moan or scream—a serious offense that they believed could even make the baby a coward. This was, therefore, one of the few times a woman might take a mild pain reliever/sedative made from willow bark (the original source of aspirin). As the contractions progressed, the women present in the birthing hut bore down with the expectant mother, imitating both mentally and physically the birth process.

When the Ojibway child was born in the traditional way, usually the birthing mother's paternal grandmother or her mother washed the baby and rubbed cedar oil on its body. Then the baby's hands were placed over its face so the baby's first breath was the scent of cedar, and it would not cry, for crying was a sign of weakness. The umbilical cord was then cut and soon burned or buried, and a tree was planted over it. Next the paternal grandmother or mother wrapped the baby in a clean blanket. The new mother removed the clothes she had worn when coming into the birthing hut and replaced them with fresh, new clothes brought by the other women. Then the traditional walk "to the west" (in a westerly direction) took place, even if the mother had to be carried most of the way. The women proceeded out of the house. The men had been waiting a respectful distance away on the path to the village or even in the village. The mother carried the baby, and her relatives followed her. She eventually handed the baby to the father, and then the two of them walked in single file with the father in the lead into or around the village. Everyone came out to witness this event, which is the way many oral traditions were and still are passed down: by people witnessing and being able to share a historical happening firsthand.

The special wigwam for this mother and her baby, and the clothes the mother wore before the birth were immediately burned by young boys appointed for this important task. This was essential for a new beginning, for a new life that had come into the world and begun its sun-path journey westward. At the appropriate time another hut was built for the next mother-to-be.

Later, a circle of rawhide with a spider web design inside was, and still is, hung over a baby's cradle to stop bad dreams and to let the good ones and the difficult ones, like lessons that had to be learned, pass through. The talisman is called a Dream Catcher.

Chapter 17

The Wedding Ceremony

According to Kee, the Ojibway translated the word "spouse" as "companion on the path of life." The translation is the same for both the man and the woman, and does not suggest one partner being superior or inferior to the other. Two people in marriage are simply companions walking together on their sun-path in a bond that is considered to be one of the strongest into which a person can enter. Traditionally, an Ojibway man is chosen for how good a provider he will be, and an Ojibway woman because of how well she will be able to provide for her family, how even-tempered she is, and whether she will be able to bear children with ease. Kee assured me, however, that young people of Indian faith are very much the same as young people from other cultures, and a person's appearance is also important to them. Nonetheless, traditional families still try to judge their possible future sons-in-law on their ability to be good providers for a family, and their future daughters-in-law to be a good companion on the road of life.

The traditional Ojibway marriage ceremony is private, personal, intimate, and for the family only. The Indian reception (a Western term) that follows is public and informal. Everyone in the village is invited, both to witness the aftermath of the event and to enjoy a day of praying, music, celebration, feasting, and gaming.

A marriage ceremony is usually held in the home of the bride's family and performed by her grandparents. The bride and groom are seated together with the other family members in a circle around them. A grandmother addresses the couple, giving the traditional oral teachings for this service: stories of loyalty, helpfulness, kindness to each other and to future children, who will, in turn, be kind to their parents. After the stories are related, the grandmother sews together the hems of the clothes the couple are wearing. During this process she speaks ritual words about looking out for one another while walking the path of life. This concludes the traditional Ojibway marriage ceremony, and the family then leaves the home or lodge to participate in the community celebration.

Given the beauty and meaning of this ceremony, my wife and I recently decided that we wished to experience such a service. We enlisted the support and help of spiritual advisor and family friend, Ed Sarabia, who agreed, after he talked at length with us, to conduct the ceremony. While the religious nature of the event prohibited pictures or videotaping, we are permitted to share the generalities of our experience.

According to tradition, the ceremony was held at our home, with only our immediate family attending as witnesses. Because it was raining hard at the time, we had to forgo the normal outdoor ceremony and instead formed a circle, holding hands, on our porch. Ed reminded us of what the circle symbolized: the cycle of life, no right and no wrong, no superior and no inferior, and no beginning and no end. Prayers were offered to the Creator for this day, the creatures of this Earth, and for our marriage ceremony. He used his abalone shell for the smudging (a purification ritual in which smoke was guided over each person's body) and then he had our oldest son, Ted, go around the circle with a pouch of untreated tobacco. Each of us, including the grandchildren, took a small amount of tobacco and held it in our hands. Ed then put some sage into the shell and lit the sage. He went inside and outside the circle to bless all of us with the smoking sage, before going around the circle and stopping in front of each of us. Aloud or silently, we offered a prayer and put the tobacco into the smoking sage, and Ed wafted the smoke around each of us with two eagle feathers. The smoke carried our thoughts and prayers to the Creator. This concluded the first part of the service, and we all moved indoors.

In our family room, we formed another circle and again offered prayers to the Creator. Our daughters-in-law, Carol and Paty Swigart, were called to bring me before Ed, and our "adopted" daughter Karen brought my angel-wife Debbie in front of him as well. He asked these ladies if they agreed to allow Debbie and me to be given away in marriage since they, as women, had created us, and thus were the only ones who could make this decision. All agreed. Ed then explained the emotional and spiritual importance of a marriage, the importance of our spiritual commitment to each other and how that must carry over to our children, whose spiritual nourishment was our responsibility. He spoke of how good and necessary it was that we protect and care for each other, adding also that we must never forget the unique soul-spirit we each brought to the marriage and which we must always nourish in each other. Next, Ed instructed us to hold hands facing him and the circle of our family, and he proceeded to wrap our hands and wrists with red and black cloth, the red cloth symbolizing our hearts and emotions, and the black symbolizing our soul-spirits. The wrapping process meant that from then on we were committed to sharing the deepest level of our being with each other. He then had us face one another and dedicate ourselves to the marriage and to each other by saying: "Share my heart. Share my life. Share my spirit."

Then we were instructed to face the circle of family, and to give the red and the black cloth to two people in the circle to symbolize our sharing of ourselves and our ceremony with others. When Ed was counseling us about the ceremony, he had told us not to predetermine to whom these would be given—the Creator would make it clear to us at the time. And the Creator did. Recognizing the struggles with major health issues that two of our family members had had during the past year and the brave way in which they had carried on during that time, we gave each of them one of our ribbons.

Ed next asked the ladies, who were still standing on either side of us, to come forward and put a blanket around us. This symbolized the ladies' acceptance and sanctioning of our marriage, and also how we would shelter each other in our married life. He then introduced us as husband and wife. He asked if anyone in the circle had anything to say to us, the newly married couple, and our children and grandchildren spoke of the example set by our love and devotion to each other and our family and what a gift this was to each of them. We all offered prayers of thanksgiving for the gift of love and family that the Creator had bestowed upon us. We then broke the circle and had a wonderful brunch, in honor of the feast that has concluded such ceremonies for as long as the oral tradition has been passed down.

Chapter 18

The "Passing Over" Ceremony

My Ojibway and other northeastern American Indian elders taught me to look at leaving this Earth—what Western culture calls "death"—as a natural process of passing over from one level of existence to another, higher one.

As I have mentioned briefly in a different context, according to Kee, when we pass over to the next life, our unique soul-spirit, which has remained separate from but within our physical self and has guided our body through our lifetime, rises from our body as we know it. This soul-spirit then begins the traditional Ojibway three- or four-day journey on the Path of Souls (the Milky Way) to the Land of Souls (Heaven). A number of world religions put forward a similar journey and destination. At the time of passing over, our soul-spirit is believed to shed itself of our physical identity. After all, as elder-teacher Ed Sarabia explained to me, we don't necessarily want always to look like we do now (or a dinosaur like a dinosaur, or a fish like a fish). We want to be free of our earthly, physical liabilities and limitations in order for our unique soul-spirit to pass on to the next level of existence and attain a new, more appropriate identity.

I feel that the way the Ojibway can approach their journey to the Land of Souls while still on Earth is wonderful. Instead of confining the critically ill patient in a hospital, continuing care facility, or bedroom separated from the normal activities of the home, I was taught by Kee that a traditional Ojibway elder or family have several options. They may decide to have a village "sing over" to help the soul-spirit of the person in question reach the next cycle, or they can have family and friends surround the person who is about to pass over and rejoice with them over what this moment means. I remember stories from my youth of elders about to pass over, propped up in bed or in a chair in the center of a room, all dressed up in their finest clothes, with the whole family there, celebrating their life and immanent journey. In addition to the traditional singing, there would be laughing, eating, drinking, dancing, and gossiping. Everyone would have a great time, including the elder who was about to pass over. All who were present would come to the elder's chair or bedside sometime during the party, not to bid a tearful goodbye, but to ask the elder to do something for them during the approaching journey and when they arrived at their appointed destination. This would allow the person left behind to have an easier time when they, in turn, had to make the same trip. These requests would concern tasks like marking the trail to help people find their way, locate their ancestors, or find the best place to settle down. No matter how critically ill and infirm the person was, they did not feel useless or abandoned, but were asked to undertake new and important responsibilities on their journey.

This may well be an apocryphal story, but my favorite tale concerning this type of activity is one I heard from a friend in northern Wisconsin many years ago. An elderly lady was very ill and had a vision, as many northeastern American Indian people do, of when she would depart to join her ancestors. A large, traditional party was set up by her family, who wished to see her off in splendid fashion. A great time was had by all, including the lady in question. And I was told the "sing over" party went on and on for more than a week, not the normal day or two. When finally asked about this by the weary family, the lady admitted she really liked parties and had exaggerated the imminence of her passing over in order to "have one last celebration." She asked what day it was, and her family gave her the date. "Two more days," she said, and the party continued for two more days, at which time she passed over, with a big smile of satisfaction on her face. Afterward, it was reported, the exhausted family and friends collapsed, and it took them several days to recover.

Given that precognitive knowledge of passing over is not a common part of our Western cultural awareness and that, with the help of prayer and modern medicine, a patient's recovery is sometimes possible, I assume these types of parties are rare today. I have never attended one, nor have any of my Indian elder-teachers mentioned attending such a ceremony. But it certainly is a wonderful concept that could, with a little creative thinking, be incorporated into our Western culture as a positive addendum to the treatment of a natural part of life that we generally accept with fear and depression.

One recent example in my own life will suffice to illustrate the power of asking a loved one who is passing over to do a favor for those left behind. I was advised several years ago by a family member that a close friend in his early eighties was terminally ill from rheumatoid arthritis of the lungs in a hospice in Florida, and would like to talk to me. I found him suffering a great deal, hardly able to talk, discouraged, and despondent. We had fished together for some thirty years with our sons in the Adirondacks, and so shared this close bond. Our conversation was necessarily brief. I reminisced about some of our more memorable and hilarious fishing times together, and ended with this admonishment: "Remember now, I'll be right behind you, so would you please find all the best places to fish? That way, when I come you can guide me. I haven't been able to fish lately, and I would really like to do that again."

When I mentioned this request he laughed, as difficult as this was for him, and he agreed, "I sure will."

As we said "so long," my friend asked me to call every other day, as this was all his failing strength and his extreme breathing difficulties would allow. During these brief calls, we always shared memories of our wonderful times together, and we looked forward to the good times we were going to have in another life because he would indeed be looking for the best fishing spots. Too soon thereafter, I could sense this would be our last conversation, and I told my friend for the first time that I loved him, for I did. His last words to me were, "I love you, Ned." According to his wife, he turned to her and said, "I love Ned," and passed over immediately.

To people of the northeastern American Indian faith, this concept of "passing over" reinforces the belief that a person's demise is not an end to their life after all, but a point on the continuum of existence to another level of peace and tranquility. This is an integral part of their faith. For those who do not follow this faith, this understanding can be, at the very least, a bright hope for all involved, as it was for my friend, a devout Episcopalian. Add to this the belief that loved ones will follow and join them, and both those about to pass over and those left behind find comfort in this. Passing over is, after all, not an end, but a new beginning.

Some Ojibway who have had a vision of their own passing are given time to complete their mission on Earth, like Del Logan and her book *Leaves of Sweet Grass*, and the famous Chief Tecumseh before his last battle, and therefore they have time to prepare for passing over. However, when passing over comes suddenly, like it did for Sitting Bull, who was shot unexpectedly by a tribal policeman at the white man's behest, people are not able to arrange their own affairs. Instead others—wives, husbands, and family members—must take over this vital process. In any case, either before or after a person has passed over, a "Give-Away Ceremony" is held. If the person is still alive, friends and family are invited, and the ill person gives them the appropriate gifts. Making the wishes of the person who will soon pass over clear while they are alive prevents potential upset and disagreements among relatives and friends concerning the deceased's possessions after that person has passed over. The custom is that the gifts are then returned to that person to use, and remain with them until the passing over of the giver, at which time the original recipients of the gifts reclaim them. This ceremony, called "Westing," has been misunderstood by white people (as have so many other Ojibway and northeastern American Indian customs), who think something is given and then taken right back. So, in a derogatory way they have labeled this practice of giving and reclaiming personal possessions "Indian giving." They do not realize that the precious belongings are only returned to the person to treasure and use during the remainder of their lifetime before becoming the property of the recipients—a wonderful concept.

For those who pass over before Westing can take place, someone very close to the departed simply fulfills the deceased person's shared or probable wishes, as for example, Sitting Bull's wife is believed to have given Frederick Remington her husband's jacket, and Del Logan's brother, Alpheus, brought us a suitcase filled with many of her personal possessions.

Also, there is great misunderstanding between some anthropologists and archaeologists and northeastern American Indian people regarding Indian possessions in burial sites that are hundreds of years old. Scientists find it difficult to believe that Indians would bury the deceased with worthless and broken objects. The small number of items also makes non-Indian scientists suspect that Indian ceremonial officials sneakily substituted these artifacts for the original ones or that they were broken to discourage grave robbers.

None of this is true. People who have passed over were buried with objects often chosen by the deceased and essential for the Ojibway's three- or four-day journey on the Path of Souls to the Land of Souls. These artifacts were broken for spiritual reasons: to free the spirit of the object and the Creator within it, so that the object would be able to accompany and serve the person on the journey along the Path of Souls. Unlike some Mayan Indian rulers of Central America, who were buried with vast quantities of material of great value for their use in the next world, Ojibway take only what they need for their short journey because it is uncertain whether they will need the objects in the Land of Souls and because material things are certainly useful to their loved ones on Earth.

Materials selected by men for their journey to the Land of Souls might include fishing and hunting gear, knives, trophies and honors from combat, or personal symbols of their clan and guardian spirits. For a woman, grave objects might include a kettle, dipper, fire-starting kit, favorite jewelry, or items a woman might take for a weekend trip.

When an Ojibway passes over, the body is washed and anointed with cedar oil, and then dressed in garments selected previously by the deceased or their family. The person is removed through the west wall of the house (or today, a window or door in traditional family homes), for this is the direction of a person's sun-path from the moment of birth until the time of passing over.

On the first day after the passing over, a grave is dug in the ground, and relatives, friends, and fellow villagers can grieve openly. Notice, even with the Ojibway and Onondaga belief in the afterlife and the return of those who have passed over to visit and advise their family and others, they cannot help but grieve for the life of a loved one or friend. However, immediate relatives are distracted by the absolute necessity, in their eyes, of providing a memorable feast for all the people who have come from near and far to witness the ceremony and pay their respects to the deceased. This feast takes place at the end of the deceased's journey on the Path of Souls—which is the close of the official mourning period.

According to Kee, in the old days Ojibway practices were quite different than they are today. The deceased's wigwam and everything that had not been given away was burned. This was an acknowledgement of the person's personal sun-path life cycle. As the birthing hut was left in ashes for the baby to begin a new life here on Mother Earth, the home of the person who had just passed over was left in ashes so they might begin a new life at a higher level of being.

A small room made of birch bark and lined with woven cedar bark was traditionally built underground in the grave to house the body of the departed and the broken artifacts that this person had chosen for their journey. The deceased was buried in a sitting position, facing west, and a "spirit house"—a miniature cabin built of bark—plus a light and a token food offering were placed on top of the grave. If any aura of the deceased person remained in the body, this aura would realize it was still loved. After three days and three nights during which volunteers kept the light burning, the last of the person's aura would be gone. There was then no need to maintain these gifts, although friends and relatives brought a symbolic food offering once a year, similar to the flowers white people put on the graves of their loved ones.

According to the Ojibway, when the journey on the Path of Souls has been completed and the soul-spirit has (presumably) passed the Creator's "balance sheet of services" and entered the Land of Souls, then the relatives and friends here on Earth are freed from grieving. How do they know the deceased has entered the Land of Souls? I have asked Ojibway people about this, and their answer was the same as mine. They were aware of the person's life and the services that were performed, and they "just knew the result." I can vouch for this because when my Dad died I remember tracking his progress across the sky at night; on the fourth day I "just knew" that my Dad had made it.

When family and friends are aware that a deceased loved one has safely reached the Land of Souls, they participate in the "Feast of the Dead." This ceremony is held to celebrate the life and the safe passage of the loved one with prayers, shared memories, and a feast of the favorite foods of that person. There are some minor differences among northeastern nations, but the concept remains largely the same. For example, the Schaghticoke Indians in Connecticut have a seven-day passing over period before the Feast of the Dead is held, but the trail and the destination are similar. I have attended these feasts and find them to be uplifting events. The remembrance food, served in a buffet line, is a gentle reminder for all who attend of the life of the person so honored. With the informality of this event, guests share heartfelt and often amusing stories about the deceased. The traditional opening ceremonies of the feast include moving tributes to the one who has passed over, and there is a sense of relief that the friends and relatives can go back to their normal lives. By tradition, however, the Ojibway wife was expected to grieve for a whole year before she was considered free of this requirement and able to return to normal life, including a possible remarriage. A husband, however, no matter how he felt personally, had to return immediately to his life of service for the good of his people.

I would like to share one more aspect of Indian burial practices. When an Ojibway person passes over, they are traditionally buried in a "Paying Back Place," a location where their physical body, which has been borrowed from Mother Earth, can be returned to Her once again. The deceased or their family might choose the location—on a hill or in the woods or in the fields—so that the deceased's remaining physical energy could be used by trees, plants, and all the living creatures of the Earth, including future human beings, as part of the continuing cycle of life.

As I have previously mentioned, one of Del's most wonderful teachings concerns the ability of a soul-spirit who has passed over to return to support, comfort, and advise us in times of special need. I can gladly relate that I have often experienced this. The return of a loved one in my dreams or even during the day is so real that I am overcome with the sense that they are truly with me—and they are!

As a matter of fact, as I was awakening one night not too long ago, Del Logan's soul-spirit came to remind me of this particular incident. In October of 1978, approximately three months after Del passed over, the phone rang in the middle of the night. Everyone dreads receiving a call at this time because it almost always means someone in the family has a major emergency that cannot wait until morning. I awakened, turned on the light, and picked up the phone. I can still remember every word of this conversation:

"Hi, Ned, it's me!" (Del's signature greeting.)

"Del, you're supposed to be dead!"

Her typical amused chuckle, followed by, "Come on, Ned, you know better than that. I just thought I'd give you a call to tell you I'll always be here for you whenever you need me."

"But, Del, by telephone? How can you?"

"Hey, didn't I always say we live in the twentieth century too? Bye!" (Her typical way of signing off).

"Goodbye, Del. We love you."

A dial tone.

I hung up and turned to face my wife.

"Who was it?" she asked.

"It was Del."

I rolled over, turned out the light, and went back to sleep. A dream? Some might choose to explain it that way. Or a dramatic example of a soul-spirit returning? To me it was the latter—absolutely.

A year later, several Native American friends were sitting with my wife and me at a mutual friend's house before dinner, and I shared this story. A Narragansett lady, Ella Thomas Sekatau, one of my elder-teachers and a friend of ours and Del's, started to laugh, saying, "Of course, it was Del. Why not? How can you doubt it?"

"But by telephone?"

Her answer was the same as Del's.

"We live in the twentieth century too, you know."

There was another remarkable incident involving Del almost two years after she passed over. Her brother, in poor health and very elderly, drove all the way from the Onondaga Reservation in Nedrow, New York, and arrived at the Institute, unannounced and unexpected. In a few words Alpheus explained his mission: to bring my family—in love—the bag Del always used when she came to visit us. He knew she would have wanted us to have it and so had saved it for us. He couldn't bring it sooner; he had been seriously ill and had had to wait until he was well enough to travel.

The small suitcase was filled with personal belongings. Such a treasure! We, with our children, reverently opened the bag and before us were such items as the beaded combs Del wore in her hair and the dress she often wore for special occasions. She had made this dress herself from the yearly federal allowance of fabric, and she had frequently used it as a visual lesson of how the US government still thought of Native Americans. A number of other personal items that we had seen so often were also there, packed carefully, as if in anticipation of an upcoming visit to our home. These were truly precious objects, made sacred by Del's use of them. As we went through her possessions, Del's image in the room with us was so real it was as if we could reach out and touch her. How could we look at her dress and her combs and not see Del wearing them, visiting us even then, and, with her classic one-sided grin, daring us to refute her presence? With the bag apparently empty, I searched once more to be absolutely sure nothing remained. Tucked away in a small end-pocket that I had not noticed before was an object that shocked us all.

I had had a precious possession, a gift that I wore all the time, a bolo tie featuring a delicate, silver and turquoise, antique Thunderbird pin made long ago in the traditional Navaho style. I was devastated when our Brittany puppy somehow found this pin and chewed it up. For all the intervening years, I had been asking our Navaho foster son Larry, Del, and every other appropriate person I could think of if they could find a similar pin for me. No one had had any success. This type of Thunderbird pin, fashioned in the Old Way, was simply not made anymore, nor could we find a second-hand one. Yet here it was, carefully tucked away in a hidden pocket in Del's suitcase—the same Thunderbird pin as my missing one—a final precious reminder of her love and her presence. Del had not had one that I knew of before she passed over; I had asked her several times over the years, and she always said she had not found one. Where had this Thunderbird pin come from, how and when was it placed in her bag, and why was it in this hidden pocket? Had Del intended to surprise me with it on her next visit? Knowing her as we did, this did not seem likely; and, according to her brother, the bag had been unopened since she last used it when visiting us. This whole idea defies logic, but if there is something I have learned over the years, it is that anything can happen—and usually does—if it is "meant to be." A friend converted the Thunderbird pin into a bolo like my original, and when I wear it for special occasions, I think of Del.

In conclusion, why is this concept of the whole process of passing over and our soul-spirit journey to a higher level of being so comforting to me in a culture that finds death so frightening? It is because it makes good sense to me, given my life experience and scientific knowledge; and like so many other northeastern American Indian beliefs, it is a positive way of looking at our role on Mother Earth. How could one not be comforted by the Ojibway, Onondaga, and northeastern American Indian description of the Land of Souls where we shall be in the future? After all, this is a place of eternal happiness and eternal summer. There is no sickness, no pain, and no sorrow; there are no hardships. The spirits of our ancestors await our arrival and welcome us with a great celebration. And we are promised we will be able to descend to Earth to visit our loved ones who have not yet joined us at this higher level of existence.

We have now come to the end of this part of today's tour, my friends, but before we move on to our next adventure, let me now share with you a beautiful poem by an unknown Native American, a poem summarizing the gift of the northeastern American Indian faith and the omnipresence of the Creator and Mother Earth in our lives.

Native American Prayer

I give you one thought to keep.
I am with you still. I do not sleep.
I am a thousand winds that blow.
I am the diamond's glint on snow.
I am the sunlight on ripened grain.
I am the gentle autumn rain.
When you awaken in the morning's hush,
I am the swift, uplifting rush
of quiet birds in circled flight.
I am the soft stars that shine at night.
Do not think of me as gone.
I am with you still...in each new dawn.

Chapter 19

The Institute for American Indian Studies: A Product of Faith, Miracles, and Human Angels

Now that you are aware of and understand the world-view represented by the northeastern American Indian faith and life, from this perspective I can share the amazing story of the birth and growth of the Institute for American Indian Studies that began with my vision thirty-nine years ago. I will share only a few examples to illustrate that if a project is Creator-inspired and is truly "meant to be," miracles happen and human angels enter our lives at the most propitious times.

Let us adjourn to our exhibit-multimedia room, where we can sit down and be comfortable while I relate this story.

1. The Involvement of Native American People

First and foremost, if we—the board, members, and supporters—ever hoped to build the Indian Institute that my vision called for, I felt it was imperative that the spiritual support and the enthusiastic backing of the Native American community be enlisted. After all, it was *their* culture, *their* faith, and, yes, *their* institute that we hoped to share with them! As with all things in a Creator-inspired project, this almost immediately came about. It all began one late-summer day in 1971, a year after my vision, when a friend stopped by our family vacation cabin in the Adirondacks in northern New York State and showed me a book he had found in his town library on Indian-related places to visit in the region. He thought I would be particularly interested in seeing a restored Iroquois village and museum in Owasko, New York. This place immediately jumped out at me as a possible example of the model I already had in my imagination to develop in Connecticut.

Several days later I awoke very early. It was cold and overcast, and the rain beat steadily on the roof over our heads. There was little to do around our cabin on such a day, and I decided to make a spontaneous trip to Owasko. I arrived early, thinking the museum would be open. It wasn't, and so, the hard rain having propitiously stopped, I drifted out to the restored village to look around. The sole person in the village, a woman clearly of Indian descent, was working industriously on some project. I wandered over and introduced myself. The lady was Adelphena Logan, who lived on the Onondaga Reservation in Nedrow, New York, and who had come in early that dismal day to be undisturbed in her work.

There was a rare, instantaneous bond between us as I explained our project. From that moment on, Del became the fledgling Institute's spiritual advisor and most enthusiastic backer. I later learned that she was a noted traditional Onondaga Iroquois historian among her people, and she was well-respected in the white world as well, serving on the boards of trustees of the Cayuga County Museum; Channel 24 Educational Television in Syracuse, New York; and the New York State Board of Indian Achievement on State Relations with Indians. She had also been the Woodland Indian Representative on President Nixon's twelve-member Commission on Indian Awareness and, shortly before her passing over, she served with me on the advisory board of the Heye Foundation's Museum of the American Indian, later to become part of the Smithsonian Museum complex in Washington, DC. She was, in fact, in charge of the Owasko reconstructed Iroquois village and exhibits that I had come to visit. Her qualifications among white and Indian alike added an immediate sense of legitimacy to our cause, and many northeastern and other Native Americans quickly became involved. Del was our first Native American board member and attended every important Institute function during her remaining days here on our Mother Earth. I can still visualize her, regal in her traditional dress made of government trade cloth, opening all of our gatherings with her traditional Onondaga Prayer, reminding us of our place in the Creator's world:

O Great Creator
whose voice I always listen for in the winds,
hear me—I am small—part of you—I need wisdom.
Let me walk in your beauty,
make my hands respect the things you have made,
keep my ears ever sharp for your voice,
help me to travel a Path of Wisdom, so I may
understand all people.
I seek knowledge—not to be greater than my brother,
but to learn to share a greater understanding.
Make me always helpful and ready to come to all
earthly causes with clean hands and clean thoughts.
Ah-Ho [Amen].

2. Local and Regional Support

After enlisting the essential support of the Native American community, the next step in our plan for the creation of the Institute was to build a local and regional base of "people power," with their potential volunteer and financial backing. This too came about through a series of propitious events. Beginning in 1965, Sidney Hessel and I, and five other diehard diggers, felt so strongly about attempting to learn more about local and regional Indian prehistory (largely unknown at the time) that we decided to do something about it. We arranged to meet two or three mornings a week to excavate a known Indian campsite on the Shepaug River in Washington, Connecticut. We did this with varying success until 1971, the summer after my vision. (Note the timing here, and the fact that this was the same year I met Del). Early that summer we had largely completed our work on a two-acre terrace hemmed in almost completely by steep hills on two sides, a brook on a third, and the Shepaug River on the fourth. We surveyed the entire site once more, hoping, but not expecting, to locate a possible new area to examine in order to complete our study there before we moved to another location. On a small lower terrace that we had already briefly tested with little success, our group of seven hit an unexpected bonanza of largely undisturbed archaeological material representing a number of different cultures. On a series of levels below the topsoil, we discovered what were apparently the first dwelling plans (with appropriate artifacts) found and recorded in New England dating back to approximately 1200 and 1500 BC. When word of our discoveries got out, the number of volunteers anxious to help skyrocketed to over 300. As many as sixty people at a time were now showing up, and we were excavating five mornings a week. We even established a baby-sitting service for grade school–aged children, and one mother appeared regularly with her infant strapped to her back in typical Indian fashion. Northeastern state archaeologists, and professionals in archaeology, soils, geology, botany, and other related fields flooded the site to see and verify our findings and to assist us in any way they could. So much regional interest was generated that a group of area citizens, including Sid Hessel and me, organized the Wappinger Chapter of the Archaeological Society of Connecticut in the early fall of that year to provide ongoing monthly programs. Later in the fall this same group decided to became a private, tax-exempt, non-profit organization—the Shepaug Valley Archaeological Society—so that we might raise tax-deductible monies to fund our rapidly developing plans to establish an Indian museum and research center.

3. The "Perfect" Location

Another vital effort at this early stage of our development was to find as perfect a location as possible for such a center. Unlike the few similar museums I was able to locate and visit, which were generally surrounded by urban life, fast food restaurants, telephone poles, and traffic, our site and surroundings had to be as pristine as possible. We wanted to ensure that visitors would be immersed in the pre-white world of nature from the moment they stepped out of their cars. Everyone agreed that the best spot to ensure this environment was a piece of land bordering the Steep Rock Reservation, a then 1,700-acre (now over 4,000-acre) privately owned wilderness park in the town of Washington, Connecticut. All of our efforts to secure our dream site were frustrated, and just when we were about to give up hope, another extraordinary event occurred. I was at a local gathering early in 1972 when the daughter of a long-time Washington resident asked to speak to me for a moment in private. She shared with me for the first time that her family was of Cherokee descent and, knowing that we were looking for protected land bordering Steep Rock, she told me how pleased and proud she would be to have the museum on property that her family and now she owned off Curtis Road. This consisted of a fifteen-acre plot of beautiful, undeveloped land on a primitive dirt road overlooking the Shepaug River Valley and bordering the Steep Rock Reservation wilderness land on her property's long western boundary. When checked for Indian occupation before construction could begin, the site was found to contain artifacts that dated back 4,000 years (the same discovery we made in our garden the year after my vision)! As if to eliminate any question about the perfection of the site, an extremely rare rock shelter made by a glacial boulder and showing signs of many years of occupation was also present on Steep Rock property immediately adjacent to our land.

The dream location for our Institute on land occupied by pre-white-contact Indians, owned by a person whose family was of Indian descent, adjoining a large expanse of forever-wild property containing a major river, and only one-half mile from my house—what are the odds of finding such a location with all of these qualities at exactly the right time?

4. The Effort to Raise Money

At the same time as these events were transpiring, we had, of course, to get down to the serious business of raising the money ($300,000) to construct and endow our extraordinary building. Another human angel, Les Searle, had devoted two years to visiting other museums nation-wide and developed what later became an award-winning plan—a wigwam-teepee style, circular building. As with everything else connected to this project, our fundraising efforts were astoundingly serendipitous. One of the many hundreds of calls that I conducted involved a top-level business executive for a major publishing company. She made it plain that I was essentially wasting my time if I wished for a financial contribution, as: "This type of project isn't part of our company's giving priorities." This was a common excuse that corporate executives offered to free themselves from yet another fundraising interview. I went to meet her anyway. I always went in faith, trusting in the Creator's Will. When I walked into her office, the executive, as white as her walls, rose from behind her desk and asked in a low voice, "Do you know there are three Indians behind you?" She was obviously shaken, and she later related that she had never had an experience like this before and was mystified. Slightly taken aback by her unexpected greeting, but aware that anything was possible, I looked, saw nothing, and asked the lady to describe these three figures. The first, she said, was right behind me, a tall white Indian dressed in white. This figure I recognized as the white Indian of northeastern American Indian mythology, similar to the white buffalo of the plains, a symbol that a mystical but real event of great importance was occurring or would occur in the near future. On my left, she said, was a heavy-set, elderly Indian woman in a brightly colored, trade-cloth dress—a description that closely resembled Del Logan. The third, another Indian woman, was also heavy set but slightly shorter and dressed in buckskin. This fit the description of Anna Escanaba, the Ojibway mother of the family I knew from my youth.

This was not the last amazing event I would experience during my fundraising ventures, but this particular vision was especially dramatic because it was the first time a vision of three Indians had occurred during my fundraising visits (it happened again), and because it was witnessed by a professional, corporate woman with little or no knowledge of this kind of Indian mysticism. Needless to say, her corporation has been very helpful in a number of different areas over the years.

5. Gaining National and International Attention

As I have mentioned, we had the involvement of the Native American community and broad-based, regional public interest in our project. Next it was essential that we earn credibility on the world scene through our archaeological excavations on the Shepaug River and other area sites.

Of course, another miracle happened. Only two years after the Institute opened to the public, our summer field school archaeologists excavated a small Paleo-Indian campsite carbon dated to 10,190 years BP (before the present) in the third square of the first randomly selected test pit in the middle of a large field, where the river flowed over 10,000 years ago. Fortunately for us, in this square a Paleo-Indian man had sat on a rock where a stream entered the Shepaug River, and made what we presumed were the items most necessary for survival and daily living. Some were broken during construction and discarded. Concentrated debris left from this process was located within only five one-meter squares from where he sat. We even found two miniature fluted points, perhaps religious items or small weapon-points. This campsite turned out to be one of the few undisturbed Paleo-Indian sites in New England and may have been the first to belong to a single-family or small extended one. The site was an archaeological and historical gold mine. Publicity about the discovery received national and worldwide newspaper and television coverage. We began to receive membership applications and visits from scientists and people from all over the world!

6. Attracting Visitors with an Extraordinary Exhibit

We moved approximately a half million Indian artifacts and other items almost entirely from Connecticut into our new center on July 1, 1975. Our immediate concern was how to attract the number of people we hoped would visit our Institute to learn about Indian faith and culture. Again, something "miraculous" arose almost immediately—it was the brainchild of our first director, Dr. Richard W. Davis, who came to the Indian Institute in 1976. He remembered hearing some time before about a nearly complete mastodon skeleton that had been excavated by Yale's Peabody Museum personnel in 1911 at the estate of A.A. Pope near Farmington, Connecticut. To Dick, showing this mastodon at Institute sounded like the perfect answer to our exhibit dilemma, but where and in what condition was it? After much searching, Dick learned that the bones had been rediscovered in their original dilapidated boxes in the "catacombs" of the Peabody Museum in New Haven. A number of bones were in varying states of decay. Apparently little if anything had been done to preserve them since their excavation in 1911. After a year of frenzied activity, the Indian Institute received a grant to properly preserve the bones and arranged a loan agreement with the State of Connecticut, which owned the material stored at the Peabody Museum. Indian Institute staff member Sharon Turner designed a creative exhibit involving the display of the bones on large sections of corrugated cardboard, piled up at various heights, to simulate an archaeological excavation. On August 6, 1977, Connecticut's only existing mastodon went on exhibit at our Visitor Center amidst much fanfare, much publicity, and a huge wave of new visitors. In a year of almost perfect coordination, with key people showing up at every turn, our dream exhibit became a reality. During the years the mastodon was on display here, it remained an outstanding attraction for visitors from all over the world.

Also, in an extraordinary coincidence, the mastodon exhibit opening took place the same year as our discovery and excavation in Washington Depot, two miles from our Institute, of the "in situ" (undisturbed) Paleo-Indian site that I described earlier. As the earliest people believed to have migrated into Connecticut, the residents of this site may well have been present during the time that our mastodon roamed the Connecticut hills and could have hunted it for food, as they had in other areas of the United States. The combination was ideal: a campsite occupied by the earliest people known in New England found by our research crews, and the mammal present during approximately the same early time in Connecticut history, found, restored, and put on exhibit by the Indian Institute staff and volunteers. Another coincidence? It doesn't seem likely to me.

7. The Indian Village and Garden, and the Origin of Corn

At approximately the same time as the Paleo-Indian and mastodon projects were taking place, the Institute's Indian staff and consultants began building a traditional pre-white Indian village, using replicas of pre-white, northeastern American Indian stone tools to authenticate its appearance and to study the efficiency of using such tools in the construction process. The Indian garden associated with the village was planted in the Old Way by our Native American staff, as I have previously discussed. Initially it flourished. Then several years later, while the rest of the garden prospered, the corn barely came up, and there was much consternation on the part of the education staff in charge of this facility. Our quarterly Native American advisory meeting was scheduled for later in the summer, and as director of the Institute at the time, I was kindly invited to sit in on this meeting. The day before it was to be held, an old friend, Dr. Richard S. "Scotty" MacNeish, called to say he was going to take advantage of a long-standing invitation and stop by to visit us and the Indian Institute that weekend. Scotty was associated with the Peabody Museum in Andover, Massachusetts. He was a noted scientist, archaeologist, and author who had helped discover and had written extensively on the origins of maize (corn) in the western hemisphere. He was participating in ongoing research on this subject in Mexico. I immediately called the chair of our Native American advisory committee to ask if Scotty could attend the meeting with me and permission was granted.

The next morning one of the first items on the agenda was the "corn problem." With profuse apologies and considerable chagrin, the Native American head of our Native American studies program told the group what had happened. The corn never grew. It was so small and stunted that she was embarrassed and had pulled it up and thrown it into the neighboring woods. Scotty asked if he could see this corn. At the meeting's conclusion, we all left the building and hurried to the garden. After a diligent search—for the offending plants had been well scattered outside the garden—samples of the corn plants were handed to Scotty for inspection. With his magnifying glass, he briefly examined the dried out, brown weeds with what looked like miniature, naked corn cobs (approximately three-quarters of an inch long), and then the explanation tumbled out. We had obtained our flint corn kernels planted in our garden from Old Sturbridge Village, a late eighteenth-, early nineteenth-century replicated small town, and in one generation in our garden the corn plants had genetically returned from the normal six-inch ear of corn used by Indians and whites alike back to the original grass from which the Indians had developed modern corn several thousand years ago. "Look here," Scotty had directed us, "there is the same number of double rows of kernels that we find in corn today, but no sheath—that would come later as Indians developed our modern corn."

He explained that the ear he was holding was the same size as the earliest carbonized cobs he had found in Mexico and that corn has the ability to genetically revert to an earlier variety, but he had "never seen anything like this before." It was his first glimpse of the original grass-corn plant in living form. Scotty passed over soon afterwards. Fortunately we kept a specimen of that grass-corn plant at the museum for all to see and study, and perhaps for some future scientists to examine. The grass-corn is also a precious memory of a special day in the lives of those who participated in this unique discovery.

Eighteenth-century Northeastern
American Indian Toboggan

8. The Artifact Collection

Numerous extraordinary items have been given to our collections over the years in dramatic fashion, for example, a birch bark canoe made in the Old Way by the Cree, and a very rare eighteenth-century Indian toboggan found in the attic of a house of that period in northwestern Connecticut by

Dr. Docksteader, director of the Museum of the American Indian in New York. Also donated was a set of European-produced powdered paints used by the Indians after white contact. I'll share one of these stories with you—that of the acquisition of the paints, which is truly remarkable. Our curator at the time, Ann McMullen, PhD, now curator for the new Smithsonian Indian Museum in Washington, DC, was involved in a study of nineteenth- and early twentieth-century Indian baskets. The results of these studies, *A Key into the Language of Wood Splint Baskets,* was published with a grant from the National Endowment for the Humanities in 1986 and republished by the Mohegan Nation in 2005 for their and our use. I will let Ann tell this story in her own words as much as possible:

> Early twentieth-century studies of woodsplint basketry decoration yielded lists of plants that were said to have been used for painting baskets. But in experiments conducted at the Institute it was found that the majority of these plants—such as bloodroot and pokeweed—yield only pale washes which do not replicate the colors seen on nineteenth-century baskets. Walnut or butternut stain seemed to be the only exceptions to this discovery.
>
> During an examination of Algonquin baskets, it was noted that a number showed evidence of vibrant colors reminiscent of those used in early nineteenth-century New England landscape paintings, house painting and furniture decorations. When compared to cakes of paint from a late eighteenth-century watercolor kit, the colors proved identical. Thus it would appear that, while Native Americans did use some natural vegetable and mineral pigments to decorate wood-splint baskets [after colonial contact], most of the colors that are preserved were of commercial origin.[25]

Ann wrote me a note explaining further: "In August of 1983, I was working hard trying to substantiate my claim that Native American basket makers used commercially produced pigments rather than the vegetable dyes or paints....I spent several days phoning paint companies and chemical supply companies trying to find samples of nineteenth-century pigments I'd read about. That week I received a phone call from a couple who had a set of Plains Indian artifacts collected by their uncle who was a bishop of the Dakota [Sioux] in the early 1900s."[26]

On the day she was telephoning museums to find out if they had a collection of such paint samples, a couple arrived at the Indian Institute with several paper bags, as I recall. In Ann's own words: "Among the beaded artifacts was what we believe is a Dakota parfleche [leather-wrapped] painting kit of commercial pigments used in the 1870s. Use of contaminated bits of the paint kit allowed us to recreate the original paint colors, which could then be matched with baskets to identify the pigments used."[27]

Not only was the timing of this gift remarkable, but the paint kit was also an unexpected surprise. Add to this the fact that this paint kit is the only such example of paints from the 1870s wrapped in the Indian manner that I know of in any museum in the country at the time. As a reminder of this special gift, Ann wove a small basket for me using samples of each color, identified on the bottom splints.

As you can clearly see from the few of many illustrations I have chosen to share with you, miracles do happen and human angels do appear in a Creator-inspired project like the Institute. These happenings immeasurably helped the Institute to come into being and ensured its continued success in offering an alternative way to view our world in a time of global social, religious, political, and environmental crises—which was our goal in its creation. Thousands of people of all ages, nationalities, and faiths from all over the world and visitors from the fifty states have now come, as you have today, to learn about our traditional northeastern Native American brothers and sisters and how they faithfully serve the Creator as stewards of all human beings and all of life on our Planet Earth. Miracles and human angels can be a part of your life. Never despair of doing important work, for you too have Creator-inspired work to do.

This completes our tour, my friends. We invite you to explore our other indoor and outdoor facilities and exhibits for as long as you wish. You might want to see one of our educational films or go outside and walk through our village and garden, our recreated archaeological dig, and our habitat trails with identified trees and plants that the northeastern American Indians used for food and for medicinal, technological, and religious purposes.

Thank you for coming to our Institute and participating in this tour. I pray that you will take the message of this holy place with you to share with all who might listen. Help us to spread the "good news" of the traditions and culture of northeastern American Indians which can add such understanding, meaningful guidance, serenity, and peace to our own lives and through us to our troubled world.

Chapter 20

Life after the Institute and a New Creator-inspired Project

In 1989 I retired from all responsibilities at the Indian Institute, secure in my own mind that the vision I had was now well established, and that this was the right time to step down. Program-, facility-, and finance-wise, the Institute was in a strong position, and at the time, the ideal candidate was ready to take over for me. Susan Payne had served the Institute in a number of important roles with great success almost since its inception, and she was familiar with all of the vagaries of its operation. Confident of the future of Institute without me and eager to return to "civilian life" free of the pressures and uncertainties of my seven-day a week, twenty-four-hour-a-day schedule of administrative and fundraising responsibilities, I passed leadership to Susan.

Even so, the change took some adjustment, particularly in the first few months. When one can see the successful launching and growth of such a project, there is an expansive sense of well-being matched by exhaustion, relief, and a certain restlessness.

After a year or two, I became resigned–contented with my new life. Yet I also began dreaming of the possibility of another exciting and challenging period of service to the Creator while simultaneously half-believing, at the other extreme, that I had successfully finished what I was meant to do and was now free at some point in the not-too-distant future to pass over to a higher level of existence as part of my life-plan.

Then, fifteen years later, after my debilitating heart attack and when I had convinced myself I would not be able to undertake another greater-than-life project, but must be content with my myriad daily blessings, "it" happened again. It was another and totally unexpected "revelation"—and it led me to what I believe with all my heart to be my latest and perhaps greatest calling: the Creator-inspired and supported writing of this book.

As for the timing of this new miracle, during the years following my resignation from leadership at the Indian Institute and before this revelation, I had experienced a long series of physical problems that made normal activities increasingly difficult, but from which I would eventually recover. In hindsight, these events were meant to more and more strongly advise me that I was increasingly straying from my unique life path—what I would call a "yellow-light sequence."

Finally, after all of the yellow-light warning signs were uncharacteristically ignored by me, the red light—the "big one"— occurred. This got my attention! In early January of the year 2000, I suffered what should have been terminal congestive heart failure. My heart simply stopped beating. The fact that I had survived over fifty previous instances of this same condition over a two-year period (despite extensive medical attention) and that my heart had restarted almost immediately each time was itself a miracle. However, surviving this final, severe episode would not have been possible but for the immediate appearance of a group of human angels. My son Ted, who lives next door and "happened" to have the day off, rushed over to help my wife; and a state trooper, who "happened" to be passing by our residence, came up the driveway and began initial treatment. Next, literally within minutes, our local volunteer ambulance, whose crew "happened" to be cleaning the ambulance at the time, arrived. Waiting for me outside the hospital emergency room was our primary physician, who had left his office and waiting patients to rush to the hospital to connect me to the heart monitor that kept my heart beating until a cardiologist could operate to make my heart continue to beat.

This event left me severely disabled, needing to rest a great deal, unable to do any but the lightest physical activities around our home, and in the beginning having difficulty remembering and expressing words and thoughts.

As my health continued to stabilize and improve, however, I became aware that visitors were asking me if the unusual story of my faith and the experiences associated with my life and the creation of the Institute for American Indian Studies was written down. On each occasion I would respond that I had always wanted to share this story but had not written it because I "had never had the time," and I would feel the painful reality that perhaps it was too late. My mental and physical condition precluded my recording it. However, my Indian faith came to my rescue. I began to realize that I had survived for a reason, for some still unrealized service for the Creator; but I had no clear suggestion of what this was. Two years passed with no resolution of my dilemma. Then, as with so many events in my life, two human angels I barely knew learned of my plight and presented me with a proposal. To rescue even a few pages of what they felt was an invaluable history which could so easily be lost, they offered to tape what part of the story of my northeastern American Indian faith I could still articulate on the days when I was well enough to try to do this. They would transcribe the taped material and return it to me for corroboration and correction. I accepted their offer with gratitude and a new sense of purpose.

When I was having a good day, my wife would call this couple, and they would come to see me if they could. They literally nursed me through the earliest of my most difficult months, asking me questions and pursuing leads until—with my limited abilities—we could go no further. They informed me that they had enough material for a pamphlet.

Miraculously, within a few weeks I suddenly regained most of my speech and thought processes, and the two returned to help me to the next level—a monograph-length story. Shortly thereafter my wife and I went away for three weeks of much-needed rest and recuperation on Cape Cod, and in the second week there my normal level of organizational skills and my ability to transcribe my thoughts on my own came back. Very excited, I called these two human angels when we returned from the Cape. Now at last we could all see where this three-year process was leading! My last congestive heart trouble, as terrible an event as it initially had seemed, was indeed a necessary part of the Creator's future plan for me. Through this final serious attack and the resulting major disabilities, the Creator had granted me the gift of "leisure time" here on Earth that I had always dreamed of having during my years of what seemed a non-stop work schedule. This respite finally offered the opportunity for me to turn inward to my soul-spirit and, with what I saw and learned there, to turn outward and, with the Creator's permission and blessing, to share with anyone who might listen, this story of my northeastern American Indian faith and the vision-creation of the Institute for American Indian Studies. Without a major health problem, this quest would have been impossible for me, as I would have continued to lead my very active life, filled with the distractions of civic, family, and house and property projects, and the constant flood of unnecessary undertakings that seems to fill every waking moment of so many of our lives.

In 2009, thirty-nine years after my initial vision and having lived to witness both the Institute for American Indian Studies and this book become a reality, I see with my Indian perspective that no undertaking is impossible, no matter how old one is, *if* it is the Creator's Will.

Epilogue:
The Circle of Life

On an evening in late August of 1972, Del and our family were sitting together in a close semi-circle around an open fire in a rustic cabin in the wilderness of upper New York State. We welcomed the fire's gift of heat on a cold, late-summer evening. As was our way with Del on such occasions, we were quiet as we all stared into the ever-changing shapes of the flames licking the dry wood, each lost in our own thoughts. Suddenly Del leaned back, ever-present teacup in hand, and with a serene smile I had never seen before, she spoke an extraordinary prophecy: "You, Ned, are the immortality of my people. You will share the Indian Way."

This book is a fulfillment of Del's prophecy.

References

1. Trudie Lamb Richmond, "The Power of the Word—The Oral Tradition." *Artifacts*, 1979. Washington, CT: Institute for American Indian Studies.

2. Adelphena Logan, *Memories of Sweet Grass*. Washington, CT: Institute for American Indian Studies, 1979.

3 "The Land." Brochure published by the Institute for American Indian Studies, Washington, CT.

4. Adelphena Logan. *Ibid.*, p. 29.

5. Trudie Lamb Richmond, "Squaw Sachems, Women Who Rule," Vol. IX, No. 2, *Artifacts,* winter/spring 1981. Washington, CT: Institute for American Indian Studies.

6. Ann McMullen, e-mail to Edmund K. Swigart, Aug 2004.

7. *Buffalo Bill Historical Center, Cody, Wyoming*. New York: Visual West, Division of Visual Books, Inc., 1977.

8. Ann McMullen, e-mail to Edmund K. Swigart, Oct 23, 2004.

9. Cleve Backster, "The Plants Respond: An Interview with Cleve Backster." *The Sun,* July 1997 (British newspaper currently owned by the News Press).

10. Keewaydinoquay, *Miniss Kitigan*, unpublished manuscript. Gardiner's Island, MI.

11. Keewaydinoquay as documented in personal notes of Edmund K. Swigart.

12. Adelphena Logan. *Ibid.*, p. 48-50.

13. Adelphena Logan. *Ibid.*, p. 18.

14. Adelphena Logan. *Ibid.*, p. 18.

15. Adelphena Logan. *Ibid.*, p. 32-33.

16. Adelphena Logan. *Ibid.*, p. 39.

17. Adelphena Logan. *Ibid.*, p. 52-53.

18. Adelphena Logan. *Ibid.*, p. 35-36.

19. Trudie Lamb Richmond, "Games of Chance and Their Religious Significance among Native Americans," *Artifacts*, Vol. VIII, No. 3, spring 1980. Washington, CT: Institute for American Indian Studies.

20. Trudie Lamb Richmond, "Walk In Harmony with the Cycle of the Seasons," Vol. VI, No. 2, *Artifacts,* winter 1977. Washington, CT: Institute for American Indian Studies.

21. Logan, Adelphena, "Authentic Indian Festival Will Be Here September 29." *Artifacts*, Vol. II, No.1, Sept 1973. Washington, CT: Institute for American Indian Studies.

22. Laurie Mac Arthur Harris, personal letter to Edmund K. Swigart, Oct 24, 2004. Litchfield, CT.

23. Maurice "Butch" Lydem, former Cultural Resource Manager of the Schaghticoke Tribal Nation, undated personal letter to Edmund K. Swigart, winter 2004. Bantam, CT.

24. Keewaydinoquay as documented in personal notes of Edmund K. Swigart.

25. Ann McMullen, "Research Brief, Pigments Used to Decorate Woodsplint Baskets." *Artifacts,* Vol. XII, No. 1, Fall 1983. Washington, CT: Institute for American Indian Studies.

26. McMullen, Ann, report to Edmund K. Swigart, director, Institute for American Indian Studies, on additions to IAIS collections, including nineteenth-century parfletches containing commercial colors and a basket purportedly made by Mollie Hatchett, undated [1984-85?]. Washington, CT: Institute for American Indian Studies.

27 *Ibid.*

Glossary

Aura—An English word defined in the *American Heritage Dictionary of the English Language* as "a distinctive air or quality that characterizes a person or thing." To Native Americans the Creator is an "Aura," an invisible cloud that created all things and surrounds and is part of all living and non-living things. An "aura" is a human invisible cloud that combines with the Aura of the Creator and is known as a "soul-spirit."

The Creator or **Great Spirit**—English words that Native Americans use to convey their sense of the Great Mystery, the force behind all Creation. To northeastern American Indians, the Creator is not in human form, but is the "Aura" or Spirit that created the universe, and that surrounds us and is part of us and of all things, both living and non-living.

Death Quest—An occurrence whereby a living person has an experience that makes them fully aware of a service they must fulfill as part of their life-path before they pass over. It is not uncommon for this person also to be told when their passing over will occur.

Give-Away Ceremony—A ceremony held when a person becomes aware of the nearness of their passing over. All their relatives and friends gather, and the person gives their possessions to the persons they wish to have them. The people who have received these gifts then return them to the donor to use until he or she passes over, at which time the recipients claim their gift. If an individual passes over before a Give-Away Ceremony, a surviving wife, husband, family member, or friend gives away the possessions based on their best knowledge of what the deceased would have done.

Medicine Man/Woman—A leader of healing services involving prayers for the body and the mind, and the dispenser of medicinal plants when appropriate. Thus the medicine man or woman fills the role of both minister and doctor in our Western society.

Miracles and **Human Angels**—Gifts from the Creator. To quote the *American Heritage Dictionary of the English Language*, a miracle is "an event that appears unexplainable by the laws of nature, and so is held to be supernatural in origin, or an act of God." A human angel, as I use the term, is not to be taken in a Christian context alone, but as a gift from the Creator-God of many religions. A human angel is a human being with special talents who appears at precisely the right time to help another human being or situation. The dictionary defines this term as a "guardian spirit or guiding influence."

Native American and **Indian**—Terms used interchangeably in this book. There are many divergent opinions about which is the preferred term.

Passing Over—An English word for an Ojibway and northeastern American Indian concept that refers to a person's journey from this Earth to a higher level of existence. The concept of "passing over" differs from our Western culture's concept of "dying," with all that word implies in Christian and other faiths.

Sacred—A word with several meanings in English, only one of which fits the northeastern American Indian way of thinking: made or declared holy. An object is not initially sacred; it becomes sacred when used by Indian people in a way that involves both the human heart and the human soul-spirit. Thus everything from untreated tobacco to the three "sacred trees" of the Ojibway and the belongings of revered chiefs are not initially sacred but become so by their use in a religious context.

Soul-Spirit—Part of, but separated from, the human body when it is alive. A soul-spirit contains the living part of human beings combined with the Creator's aura. When a human being "passes over," their soul-spirit leaves the physical body behind and passes to a higher level of existence where the physical body is no longer needed.

Tribe and **Nation**—The word "tribe" is most often used in Western society and now by many Indians as well to describe a Native American group of people sharing a common ancestry, language, culture, and name. The word "nation" reflects a more accurate description of the level of organization and self-governance that many of the tribes have or are trying to establish.

Yellow Light and **Red Light**—My own English words to describe an Ojibway and northeastern American Indian concept involving the Creator's advising someone that they are straying too far from their life-path. Yellow lights take the form of increasingly negative life events of almost any kind until, if necessary, a calamity or red light, creates a major life change to more strongly indicate the direction of a life-path.

Bibliography

Buffalo Bill Historical Center, Cody, Wyoming. New York: Visual West, Division of Visual Books, Inc., 1977.

Backster, Cleve, "The Plants Respond: An Interview with Cleve Backster." *The Sun,* July 1997 (British newspaper currently owned by the News Press).

Harris, Laurie Mac Arthur, personal letter to Edmund K. Swigart, Oct 24, 2004. Litchfield, CT.

Keewaydinoquay, recorded by "Direction We Know: Walk in Honor." Michigan: Miniss-Kitigan Drum, 1979, 9th printing, 1983.

Keewaydinoquay, *Miniss Kitigan,* unpublished manuscript. Gardiner's Island, MI.

Logan, Adelphena, *Memories of Sweet Grass.* Washington, CT: Institute for American Indian Studies, 1979.

Logan, Adelphena, "Authentic Indian Festival Will Be Here September 29." *Artifacts*, Vol. II, No.1, Sept 1973. Washington, CT: Institute for American Indian Studies.

Logan, Adelphena, "Indian Harvest Festival Is a Moving Experience," *Artifacts,* Vol. II, No. 2, Dec1973. Washington, CT: Institute for American Indian Studies.

Lydem, Maurice "Butch," former Cultural Resource Manager of the Schaghticoke Tribal Nation, undated personal letter to Edmund K. Swigart, winter 2004. Bantam, CT.

McMullen, Ann, "Research Brief, Pigments Used to Decorate Woodsplint Baskets." *Artifacts,* Vol. XII, No. 1, Fall 1983. Washington, CT: Institute for American Indian Studies.

McMullen, Ann, report to Edmund K. Swigart, director, Institute for American Indian Studies, on additions to our collections, including nineteenth-century parfletches containing commercial colors and a basket purportedly made by Mollie Hatchett, undated [1984-85?]. Washington, CT: Institute for American Indian Studies.

McMullen, Ann, e-mails to Edmund K. Swigart.

Richmond, Trudie Lamb, "The Power of the Word—The Oral Tradition." *Artifacts*, 1979. Washington, CT: Institute for American Indian Studies.

Richmond, Trudie Lamb, "Games of Chance and Their Religious Significance among Native Americans," *Artifacts*, Vol. VIII, No. 3, spring 1980. Washington, CT: Institute for American Indian Studies.

Richmond, Trudie Lamb, "Squaw Sachems, Women Who Rule," Vol. IX, No. 2, *Artifacts,* winter/spring 1981. Washington, CT: Institute for American Indian Studies.

Richmond, Trudie Lamb, "Walk In Harmony with the Cycle of the Seasons," Vol. VI, No. 2, *Artifacts,* winter 1977. Washington, CT: Institute for American Indian Studies.

Sinnott, Edmund, *Biology of the Spirit.* New York, 1955 ed., 1973 republication by Science of Mind Publishing.

Who's Who in the World. Chicago, IL: Marquis Who's Who, 1984-85,1008.

Acknowledgements

I would be remiss if I did not thank the staff that worked with me during my years at the Institute for American Indian Studies (founded as, and for many years known as, the American Indian Archaeological Institute). They were as dedicated as I was to seeing the Indian Institute become all I had prayed it would, and they have been an integral part of many of the miraculous events I have shared in this book. In this regard, I especially wish to thank: Director of the Institute Elizabeth McCormick; former Director Dr. Richard Davis and Dr. James Mooney; former Director of the Institute and former Director of the Education Department, Susan Payne; former Director of Education and of the Native American Studies Program, Trudie Lamb Richmond (Schaghticoke); former Director of Education Karen Cody Cooper (Cherokee); former Education Department staff members Ann Dukes, Barrie Kavasch, Steve Post, and Dave Richmond (Akwesasne Mohawk); former Directors of Research, Dr. Roger Moeller and Dr. Russell Handsman; former Curators Sharon Wirt, Ann McMullen, and Lynn Williamson (Mohawk); former Research Department staff members Joanne Bowen, Jane French, Roberta Hampton, and Jean Pruchnik; and former business manager Norma Went.

And how may I ever thank the thousand-plus volunteers who donated their precious time and talent to every phase of Institute life—from publications such as our newsletter, to teaching, working on archaeological "digs" and in the lab, constructing exhibits, making shop crafts, fundraising, doing mailings, heading special events, serving as tour guides and librarians, working on habitat trails and the Indian village and garden, and contributing to so many other activities. Without our volunteers' loyalty and service, we could never have achieved such immediate and long term success in our numerous ventures.

Along the way I have also met many unforgettable people without whose constant encouragement and support, my vision to found the Indian Institute would not have become a reality. Among them are Alvin Josephy, John Pawloski, Lyent Russell, and all former and present Institute Board members, including the important "early stalwarts": Co-founder of Institute Sidney Hessel, Tate Brown, Elmer Browne, Paul Bruning, Ken Green, Harlan Griswold, Ken Howell, Marie Sheehy, Lloyd Young, and initial fundraising consultant and later board member John Carlson.

I also especially wish to thank my teachers, Native American elders—knowledgeable about the "Old Way" of the oral tradition— and my scientist-elders—knowledgeable about the "New Way" of modern science. Their generous and patient sharing of their knowledge has affirmed my Indian way, my personal relationship with the Creator, my vision to found the Indian Institute, my "revelation" about writing this book, and the peace, serenity, and faith with which I am now blessed.

Native American elders I especially wish to thank include: the Maestro (Aztec); Mikki Aganstata and Karen Cody Cooper (Cherokee); Ray Fadden and Irene Richmond (Mohawk Iroquois); Gladys Tantaquidgeon (Mohegan); Ken Mynter (Mohican); Clara Addison and Ella Thomas-Sekatau (Narragansett); Anna Escanaba, Keewaydinoquay, Winona, Adam Nordwall, and "Turtle Woman" (Ojibway); Adelphena Logan, Oren Lyons, and Dewescenta (Onondaga Iroquois); "a man with no name" (Potawatomi); former Chief Irving Harris, Chief Richard Velky, and Butch Lydem (Schaghticoke); Alphonso Ortiz, Tewa, and Ed Sarabia (Tlingit).

Scientists include: former associate with the Physics Department at John's Hopkins University Dr. Donald Andrews; Connecticut State archaeologists, Dr. Douglas Jordan and Dr. Nicholas Bellantoni; former Curator of Anthropological Collections at Yale University's Peabody Museum, and former Professor of Anthropology and Director of Undergraduate Studies at Yale, Dr. Michael Coe; former New Jersey State Archeologist and Chair of the Anthropology Department at Seton

Hall University, Herbert Craft; former Director of the Heye Foundation's Museum of the American Indian in New York, Dr. Frederick Docksteader; former Acting Director of the Brooklyn Museum and former Curator of Primitive Art, Dr. Michael Kan; former Professor of Physics and Philosophy at Yale University, Dr. Henry Margenau; former staff member of the Peabody Museum, Andover, Massachusetts, Dr. Richard "Scotty" McNeish; former New York State archaeologists, Dr. William Ritchie and Dr. Robert Funk; botanist, ecologist, and former Chairman of the Yale Graduate School of Conservation, Dr. Paul Sears; former Professor of Biology at Yale University, Dr. Edmund Sinnott; and former Chairman of the Anthropology Department, Central Connecticut branch of the University of Connecticut, Dr. Fred Warner.

Of my many wonderful Native American teachers, I wish to recognize three very special individuals, who, through their knowledge, encouragement, and support over the years, have made my dream of sharing this life-journey possible. The first person is the beloved acting grandmother of our family, Adelphena "Del" Logan, an Onondaga Iroquois. At every opportune moment during the later years of her life, Del was my family's teacher. She honored us not only by sharing her abiding faith in her religion and culture, but also by giving us her most precious family heirlooms. The second is Keewaydinoquay of the Ojibway Nation. Kee was a most skilled teacher. Her knowledge of her faith, her culture, and the flora used by her people was truly encyclopedic, and her willingness to share with me the heart and soul of her Ojibway faith, was an inspiration. The third is Coordinator of Indian Affairs for the State of Connecticut, Department of Environmental Protection, Ed Sarabia, a Tlingit, born and raised. Ed is a true kindred spirit and a brother in the faith—despite that I am of European descent and he is Indian through and through. His tremendous wisdom and insight concerning the most fundamental tenets of Indian faith and his encouragement, advice, and support were vital to the writing of this book.

Additionally there is the host of people who responded so generously to help me with this project. I am especially grateful to Cel Ellerman, Linda Grigg, Laurie Harris, Carol Hart, Barrie Kavasch, Marilyn Makepiece, Paul Peschel, Vincent Pickhardt, and Alice Rismon for providing photographs and important information.

How can I forget the people who saved my life in a miraculous set of coincidences and who, with the Creator, gave me the additional time to make the writing of this book possible? Thank you to my primary physician Dr. Alphonse Altorelli, to State Policeman Ron Dirrazio, and to our volunteer ambulance crew, including Mary Anne Green and Mat Somerset.

I also wish to express my gratitude to those people who most supported, encouraged, and aided me in the preparation and publication of this book. The two people who wrote the Foreword, in addition to being my teachers, served on the staff of the Indian Institute: former Director of the Education and of the Native American Studies Programs, Trudie Lamb Richmond (Schaghticoke), and former education staff member and the person in charge of the Indian village and garden, Dave Richmond (Akwesasne Mohawk). My gratitude also is extended to editors Chez Liley and her husband, Paul Winter, of the Paul Winter Consort, Beth Brady Walker, Jane Lahr, and—during the final phase of the publication process—the very professional team of editor Jane Bernstein; photographer Heidi Johnson; designer Kate Boyer; and publisher Ann Hughes.

Finally, I wish to offer my heartfelt thanks: to my sons Ted and Paul, who have supported and encouraged me in all of my efforts on behalf of our Native American brothers and sisters and have helped to keep my vision alive by serving on the board of the Indian Institute after my retirement; to my daughter Lucie, who helped me run archaeological excavations in our early Institute days and who has always supported my many projects; and to my human angel-wife and best friend for over fifty-four years, Debbie Herold Swigart, for the extraordinary way in which she has loved, supported, and nurtured me with such serenity and grace, while still finding the time to be a wonderful mother, grandmother, sister, aunt, friend, church member, and community servant.

As an all-important addendum to this list and with great temerity and awe, I add my eternal appreciation for the presence of the Creator in every aspect of my life, guiding me, encouraging me, cajoling me, inspiring me, and accepting me for what I am—an imperfect vessel who has nonetheless been allowed the great privilege of sharing the Creator's Spirit and Wisdom as best as I can.

About the Institute for American Indian Studies

The Institute for American Indian Studies (IAIS) welcomes thousands of children and adults each year to its museum and research center. Open seven days a week year-round, the IAIS offers several feature events each weekend, including workshops, lectures, public-oriented archaeology programs, Indian-related discussions and conferences, films, craft classes, demonstrations of Indian life and technology, field trips, new exhibit receptions, and special events such as honoring Indian veterans on Veterans Day. The IAIS store is stocked with craft items, jewelry, and art from across Native America.

Widely recognized as a cultural treasure, the IAIS has received honors including the Achievement Award from the US Department of the Interior's Heritage Conservation and Recreation Service, a Phoenix Award from the Society of American Travel Writers, and a National Award of Merit from the American Association of State and Local History. For more information or to plan a visit, contact:

The Institute for American Indian Studies
Museum and Research Center
38 Curtis Road
PO Box 1260
Washington, CT
06793-0260
860-868-0518
www.birdstone.org

IAIS Co-Founder Edmund K. Swigart
and Northeastern American Indian Girl